Geographic Area Covered

Bermuda (U.K.)

THE BAHAMAS

Nassau

Turks and Caicos Islands (U.K.)

British Virgin Islands (U.K.)

DOMINICAN REPUBLIC

Port-au-Prince

Anguilla (U.K.)

ST. KITTS AND NEVIS

HAITI

Santo Domingo

Puerto Rico (U.S.)

ANTIGUA AND BARBUDA

Navassa Island (U.S.)

Guadeloupe (FR.)

Montserrat (U.K.)

DOMINICA

Martinique (FR.)

aribbean Sea

ST. LUCIA

ST. VINCENT AND THE GRENADINES

BARBADOS

Aruba

Curacao

Bonaire

GRENADA

ranquilla

Maracaibo

Port-of-Spain

tagena

Caracas

TRINIDAD AND TOBAGO

VENEZUELA

Georgetown

Medellín

GUYANA

Paramaribo

French Guiana

Bogotá

SURINAME

Cayenne

COLOMBIA

Cali

ADOR

Manaus

Iquitos

BRAZIL

Tropical & Garden
FLOWER
Identification

Graeme Teague

18 RABBIT PRESS, INC., Adel, Georgia USA

Printed In Singapore

ACKNOWLEDGEMENTS & CREDITS

PERSONAL:

From several life times worth of travel, adventure, observation, shooting and learning, finally, comes my first book, and perhaps a surprise to many—a tropical flower book!

No matter where I was living and working, I found myself either directly or subtly involved in plants and gardening, and above all, in exploring new realms of creativity for abstract art, inspired by tropical flowers. The interplay of angles, lines and blazing neon colours continues to be an intoxicating combination for my creative process.

Plants have given me solace in hard times; provided therapy, creativity, productivity, and many new friends; fostered pride of self, pride of accomplishment, pride of place; given me shade, fun, oxygen, a good sweat and a few pricks and stabs—a.k.a. wisdom!

Nothing is accomplished in life without help and support, and an undertaking such as this guide book has taxed my friends and family whose unwavering encouragement over the years has been inspirational. Input from friends and acquaintances has been both memorable and motivational. Indeed, the number of complete strangers who assisted freely of their time, simply because it involved flowers and gardening, has been truly amazing—plants bring out the best in all of us. I know I will miss many names here, and for that short-coming I apologize, but you all know who you are and I cannot thank you enough for your kindness, hospitality, support and friendship over the years.

Special Thanks To:

My parents, Bill & Yvonne Teague, for the never ending sacrifice, help, encouragement and unprecedented support throughout my entire life, including research, photos and editorial hardships with this book!

My brother John; rock steady and true.

My lifelong friend David Vaughan, who taught me to 'see' and whose design and layout of the book is both brilliant and beautiful.

Jean Weaver, whose years of support and love for our family has been selfless, and without whom the book would never have happened.

Dear friends: Gene & Leah Sherman; Robert & Jeanine Feldman; Bob & Sandy Swanson; Paul Humann and Troy Edwards and their glorious tropical home *Mango Manor*; and Helen Murphy and Miguel Acosta—for your years of belief, encouragement, friendship and support, thank you all.

First Edition 2006

ISBN 10: 0-9788730-0-9

ISBN 13: 978-0-9788730-0-4

Publisher: 18 Rabbit Press, Inc. 206 Magnolia Drive. Adel, GA. 31620
229-896-8336 • www.flowerid.com

PROFESSIONAL:

Art Direction, Layout & Design: David Vaughan; 18 Rabbit Press, Inc.

Spanish Common Name Help:
Helen Murphy; Parrot Tree Gardens, Roatan, Bay Islands, Honduras

Zulu Plant Names: Adrian Koopman; Professor of Zulu Studies; Director, Onomastic Studies Unit, Natal University, Pietermaritzburg, South Africa.

Plant Identification Help: Michael Davenport, BA.; Director, Living Collections & Garden Landscapes, Fairchild Tropical Garden, Miami, Florida, USA.

Fruit Tree Help: Mary Collins; Senior Horticulturist, Fairchild Tropical Garden, Miami, Florida, USA

Cactus Help & Identification: Daiv Freeman; www.cactiguide.com

Orchids: Gregory Basco, B.Sc.; Tropical Ecology, Alajuela, Costa Rica, Central America

Research & Plant Identification Help: Patricia Mitchum

The staff at the Fruit & Spice Park, Homestead, Florida, USA

PHOTOGRAPHY NOTES:

All images of the plants and flowers in this book were taken in their natural environment: in the wild; at tropical gardens, both public and private; nurseries; along the side of the road; and plantations around the islands. No images were set-up or shot in labs or studios.

Starting in 1977, with my first diving trip to the Cayman Islands, I was captivated by both the underwater world and tropical *terra firma* of the West Indies. The plant and flower images were taken between dives over a 25-year span in the tropical West Indies, Central America, Florida and Georgia.

Originally, equipment consisted of a single used Nikon F2 with a 55mm macro lens (that I took out of my housing), and Kodachrome 64 film. For 'wide angle' work, I used my underwater camera, a Nikonos III with a 35mm lens, and Kodachrome 64 film. Everything was fully manual!

For years, my topside work has been shot with Olympus OM4T's, and several dazzling Zuiko lenses: 16mm f3.5 , 24mm f2, 50mm macro f2, 200mm f4, and a 75-150mm f4.

Film has been Kodachrome 64 and 200, and lately Kodak E100VS.

I finished the book shooting with a Sony DSC-F717 5MP digital camera which features an astonishing 300mm Carl Zeiss lens that also does 1:1 macro perfectly, plus night vision and video with sound—and I'm checking to see if it will cook my breakfast too—fully automatic, of course!

Photography is an extraordinary medium of expression with enormous power to pull emotional responses from human beings. I love this planet and it's life and feel compelled to always use my gifts to show the very best of why it is so beautiful and worth protecting and saving. This book is a first step in showcasing the extraordinary library of moments in light and time that I have encountered over the years. Hopefully it will inspire not just gardeners and flower lovers but all people to stop, take a moment, look around, appreciate the beauty of your world, and smell the flowers.

PHOTO CREDITS:

Author's photo – Larry Benvenuti

BIG LEAF SHRUBS:
Spathe Flower – David Vaughan

DRY ENVIRONMENT:
Pineapple plantation – Greg Basco

Pineapples growing – Greg Basco

LILIES:
Spider Plant Flower – Phillip Ruttenbur

ORCHIDS:
All the orchid photography is by Greg Basco, from the rainforests of Costa Rica.
www.deepgreenphotography.com
Tours & Information:
www.fotoverdetours.com

PONDS & AQUATICS:
Golden Canna Lily – Paul Rebmann
www.wildflphoto.com

Golden Canna Lily Flower – Paul Rebmann
www.wildflphoto.com

SHRUBS:
Bird of Paradise - Mandela's Gold
– Jean Weaver

Glory Bush – Forest & Kim Starr (USGS)

Glory Bush Flowers – Forest & Kim Starr (USGS)

Yellow Elder – Josephine Keeney

Yellow Elder Flower – Forest & Kim Starr (USGS)

VINES:
Bougainvillea 01 – Jean Weaver

Chalice Vine Flower – Paul Humann

Dutchman's Pipe – Jean Weaver

TREES:
Autograph Tree Flower
– Forest & Kim Starr (USGS)

Autograph Tree Fruit
– Forest & Kim Starr (USGS)

Cannonball Tree Flowers – David Vaughan

Jacaranda – Jean Weaver

Jacaranda Flower
– Forest & Kim Starr (USGS)

Purple Orchid Tree Flower
– TopTropicals.com

Red Silk Cotton Tree 01 – James Singer

Red Silk Cotton Tree 02 – James Singer

Red Silk Cotton Flower – TopTropicals.com

Sausage Tree – Jean Weaver

Sausage Tree Fruit – Jean Weaver

White Powder Puff Tree Flower
– TopTropicals.com

Ylang-Ylang Flower – Paul Humann

TREES – FRUIT:
Ackee Fruit – TopTropicals.com

Ackee Fruit Open – TopTropicals.com

Almond Tree – Greg Basco

Almond Tree Fruit – Greg Basco

Almond Tree Flower – Greg Basco

Breadfruit Tree – Greg Basco

Breadfruit Tree Fruit
– Forest & Kim Starr (USGS)

Cacao Flower – Greg Basco

Calabash Gourd – Bill Teague

Coconut Palm – David Vaughan

Coffee Berries (full page) – David Vaughan

Cuban Band with Calabash Instruments
– Larry Benvenuti

Litchi Fruit – TopTropicals.com

Malabar Chestnut Fruit – James Singer

Malabar Chestnut Fruit (open)
– James Singer

Malay Apple Tree
– Forest & Kim Starr (USGS)

Malay Apple Fruit
– California Rare Fruit Growers, Wim Veer

Malay Apple Flower
– California Rare Fruit Growers, Wim Veer

Rose Apple Tree Fruit – TopTropicals.com

All other images (475) are by the author.
www.agpix.com/gtphoto

GRAEME TEAGUE

Family: *Teague*

Factotum universalis

Tags: *Grambo, Grae, G-man, Mafuta*

Occupiers: *Master Dive Instructor, Underwater Photographer, Hard Hat Diver, USCC Captain, Racer, Author, Gardner, Eco-Adventure Guide, Cat Person, Goey-ducker, Bartender*

There's an unwritten *"regulation"* between families in the Canadian Armed Forces whereby the offspring of military personnel are to be given food and shelter whenever they should pass through town on their worldly travels. A call comes out of the blue, always late at night and during inclement weather, and the family member closest in age to the weary traveller is sent out, grumbling, to collect him and look after him during his stay. This is how I met Graeme, some thirty-plus years ago, in Toronto. He was perched on an enormous duffel bag in the bowels of the subway, and though we had never met before and there were hundreds of other travellers milling about, we instinctively knew we were looking for each other. And so the adventures began.

Graeme was already a seasoned wayfarer, spawn of nomadic parents who had, literally, taken him to the farthest-flung corners of the Earth. Starting in Alberta, Canada, in 1959, they managed to explore the vast spaces from balmy Queensland, Australia, and Zululand, South Africa, to frigid Inuvik, 160 miles north of the Arctic Circle (where Graeme found time to invent the snow-board) and finally to Vancouver Island, British Columbia, where a love affair with all things wet and wild led him into commercial diving and underwater photography. When I found him, patiently atop his duffel full of dive gear, he was headed for the Cayman Islands with his venerable Nikons on what would become a life-long pilgrimage to the tropics, for the "waters", as they say, and as it turns out, for the "flowers" as well.

We alternated visits over the decades and experienced many memorable adventures together with too many good times to count. He saved my life, I saved his life. And always, no matter how hot or tired, no matter how remote or precarious the perch, we had 400lbs of cameras and lenses strapped to our bodies to capture it all. Graeme would have us up long before the sun, traipsing through the jungle, lost in the morning mists looking for that perfect beam of light to fall. We'd spend hours working a pile of ancient ruins, clambering into every crack and trying every goat trail.

Graeme was relentless in his quest and I'd often find myself suddenly alone. While I'd be catching my breath high above the main court of the ruins in Copan, contemplating the tranquil greens of the valley and wondering what I'd have for breakfast, he'd be adding that elusive bloom that would bring him closer to the realization of this field guide. To find him, I'd have to listen for the rather expensive sound of optical glass and brass clattering down the rocks as one of his macro lenses tumbled down the path to my feet. The surest way was to ▶

wait for his distinctive, booming laughter, legendary throughout the Caribbean, echoing across the valley and raising flocks of spooked macaws. We'd have had an entire day's adventure under our belts well before our travelling companions had even rolled out of bed.

I never realized that after thirty years of tip-toeing between nervous alligators in the Everglades, careening down rain-ravaged Honduran donkey tracks in a *tuk-tuk*, listening to killer-whales calling to each other over a car radio in Telegraph Cove, crawling inside ancient Mayan pyramids, vomiting into regulators from bad air one hundred feet underwater, racing Formula Fords in Mont Tremblant, or riding out hurricanes... that Graeme was secretly, tenaciously compiling the archive for this book. And doing it all with the gusto and *joie de vivre* that, for anyone who knows him, infuses everything he does.

This book has been a labour of love for Graeme and I know that he wishes all its readers have as much fun using it as he had bringing it to life.

David Vaughan

David and Graeme, with bemused driver, survive yet another death defying tuk-tuk ride in the jungle!

Cover: Shaving Brush Tree - *Pseudobombax ellipticum*

Back Cover: Heart of Flame - *Bromelia balansae*

Century Plant Flower - *Agave americana*

Inside Back Cover: Author's photo - David Vaughan

CONTENTS

INTRODUCTION

The ancient Persians called a walled-in garden a *"paradasa"*, from which we get the English word "paradise". The Persians derived their garden inspirations from an even earlier civilization, the Sumarians, who built the first cities ever, such as Suma, around 5000BCE, making formal gardens as ancient as civilization itself.

Ancient Egypt had gardens dating 1,500 years prior to the erection of the legendary *Hanging Gardens of Babylon*. Wealthy Romans were the first to have private gardens and landscaping for pleasure designed into their personal villas, whose function and appearance have immense appeal to this very day.

The world's greatest monument to love, the Taj Mahal, had a Persian architect whose formal gardens are a representation of the *Garden of Eden*, with a central fountain and four canals representing the four rivers of Eden. Over the entrance, the inscription reads simply, *'You Are Entering Paradise'*.

GARDENS AT VIZCAYA – MIAMI, FLORIDA

Today we clearly understand the therapeutic value of living in a "*green*" world. Practically every single human dwelling, wherever we settle around the globe, has at least one potted house plant as part of our "*nesting*" process. Gardens, plants and flowers ellicit an emotional response and are an integral part of the human spirit throughout our history.

The tropical plants and flowers occurring throughout the West Indies that appear in this book are a joy to observe, grow, and in most cases, smell. They are a smorgasbord for the senses; a pleasure for both travelers and residents alike to these areas. The intense lushness of foliage and profusion of spectacular colours is a hallmark of tropical and sub-tropical regions.

Wherever you live or travel, you are encouraged to visit tropical and formal gardens. They are full of information, ideas, pleasure and inspiration for implementing your own garden.

HOW TO USE THIS BOOK

The basic concept that formed the book was ease-of-use for everyone.

An initial guide, a starting point as both an easy to use tropical flower identification book, as well as a gardening information guide to growing tropical flowers.

Toward those goals, the plants divide naturally into twelve groups that make up the twelve chapters. The comfort of common names is used throughout with the botanical classification (in italics), Family, Genus and Species listed for positive identification of each plant.

As huge tracts of the geographical area have Spanish as their official language, Spanish Common Names are also included.

Familiarize yourself with the twelve groups so that when you observe an unknown flower or plant you can check for the basics: ask yourself, is it a vine, shrub, cactus, in a pond? What colour are the blooms, leaves, fruit? From there go to the chapter on flowering vines or flowering shrubs or dry environment or ponds and leaf through till you find your matching plant.

Because of the enormous number of species and cultivars found in the geographic region, it was impossible to do a book with every single plant included. The chapters represent a wonderful cross section of the most common to some exotic species in each group.

Your "*unknown*" flower might not match exactly at times, but the guide should steer you in the right direction to read and see how many species, similar species and cultivars are involved, which should then point you to specialized books or websites that are plant specific to your flower.

NOTES FOR GARDNERS:

Whatever exotic and wonderful tropical plant or tree you want to grow, this book serves as an initial guide. Make sure you research your choices fully before purchasing and planting. Check for growing details in your area, possible problems or diseases, and especially growing-from-seed instructions. Plan carefully, realizing final growth sizes, growth rate, sun exposure, salt, wind and cold tolerance, water, soil and food needs, indoor, outdoor and winter maintenance. Even legalities, as certain plants are protected and things like seed collecting or transporting across state borders are illegal.

The internet remains your best and easiest source for information.

BOTANICAL CLASSIFICATIONS:

The botanical classification or Latin names of plants are important to have as references since you will need to use them when doing internet searches or ordering seed, while nurseries and gardens label their plants with botanical names.

Each plant was identified by three independent sources. If there were any unresolved discrepancies during the research, I refered to the US Government Plants National Database to decide the taxonomy listing.

NOTES ON ALTERNATIVE MEDICINE:

This is not a herbal medicine guide book in any way. Many plants appearing in this book are toxic to highly toxic and are noted as such. Medicines and alternative uses are listed as informative and historical asides. There are no recipes or recommendations on using any of these plants for anything other than looking great in your garden.

BOOK REFERENCES:

Flowering Trees of Florida, Stebbins, Pineapple Press, Inc., Sarasota, Florida

Tropical Blossoms of the Caribbean, Hargreaves, Hargreaves Company, Inc., Kailua, Hawaii

Tropical Trees, Hargreaves, Ross-Hargreaves, Lahaina, Hawaii

TOP RESEARCH WEBSITES:

This is definitely a 21st century project in that the internet was used almost exclusively for the research. Although thousands of websites were used in researching and writing the book, the following sites were consistently the best overall.

Cactus Guide - *www.cactiguide.com*

Fruits of Warm Climates - *www.hort.purdue.edu/newcrop/morton/index.html*

Gardeners' plant database and information - *www.davesgarden.com*

Large plant and flower database - *www.desert-tropicals.com*

Multilingual Multiscipt Plant Name Database
- *www.plantnames.unimelb.edu.au/Sorting/List*

National Tropical Botanical Garden - *http://www.ntbg.org*

Plants and flower data - *www.floridata.com*

US Government Plants National Database - *http://plants.usda.gov*

FLOWER PARTS:

Most flowers have a ring of sepals, collectively called a calyx, and above that a ring of petals, collectively called a corolla. The anther and filament make up the stamen while the stigma, style, ovary and ovule make up the carpel or pistil. Some plants, like the milkweeds, have an additional ring of appendages that sits above the corolla like a crown, called a corona.

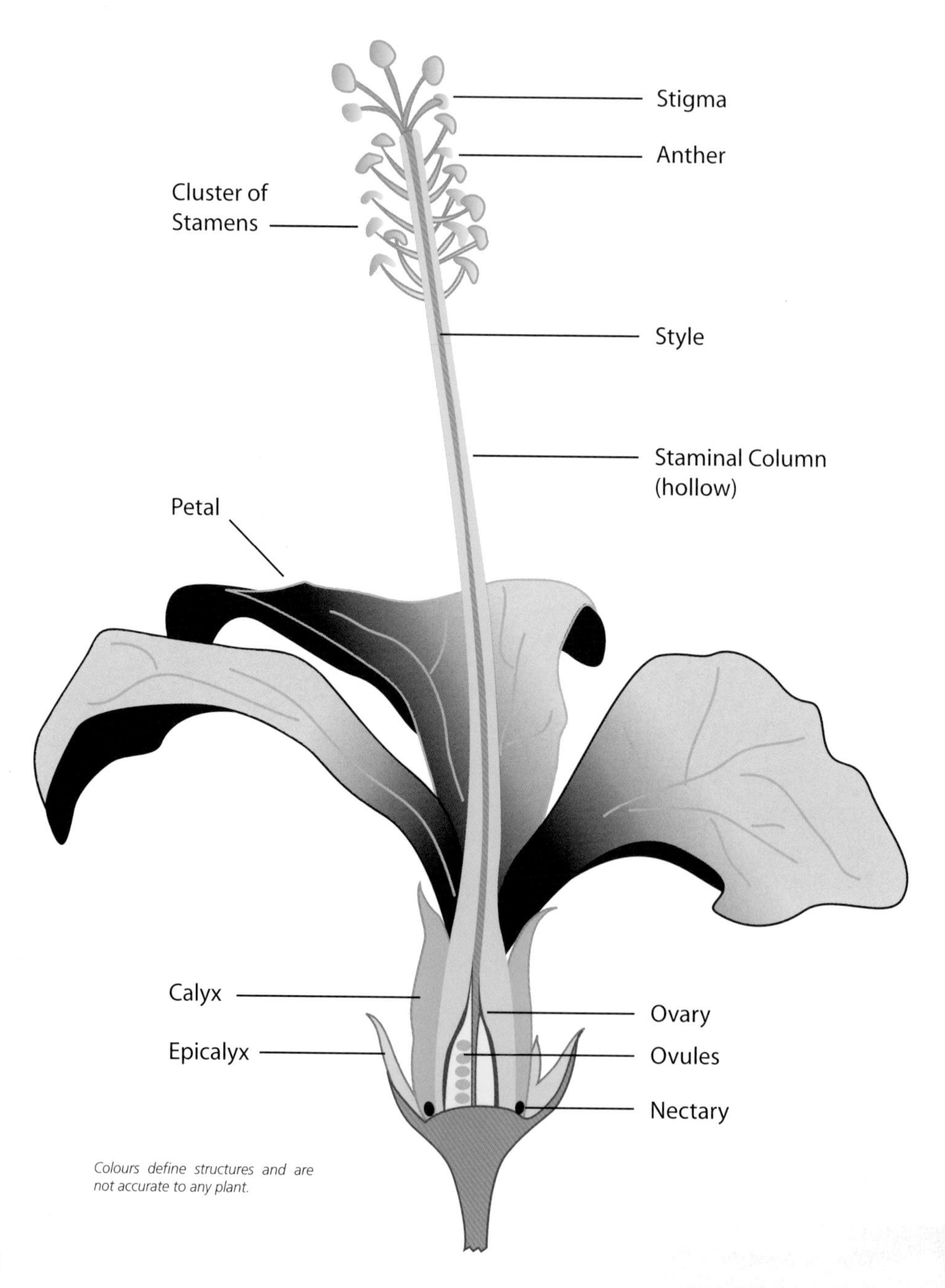

Colours define structures and are not accurate to any plant.

ELEPHANT EARS - SOUTH FLORIDA

Chapter 1
BIG LEAF SHRUBS

The Araceae are rhizomatous or tuberous herbs comprising about 110 genera and at least 1,800 species, some count as many 3,700 species, all of which vary in growing habits. Some characteristics include large leaves, climbing shrubs, epiphytic roots, tubers and rhizomes. Many species are poisonous.

The vast majority of the genera occur in the New World tropics. Members of the family are highly diverse in life forms, leaf morphology, and inflorescence characteristics. The family is best characterized by its distinctive inflorescence, a spadix with and subtended by a solitary spathe on a long or very short peduncle. The flowers are often enclosed in the leaf-like spathe which can be brightly coloured. Its leaves are often broad with netted venation or parallel-veined leaves. Wherever you are in the world, if you see these patterns you can be pretty sure you are looking at a member of the Araceae.

Some, like the small Anthurium andreanum, grown for the long-lasting flowers and associated bracts, are popular in floral arrangements and are a significant commercial crop, especially in Hawaii.

ANTHURIUMS

Family: *Araceae*

Anthurium andraeanum

English: *Tail Flower, Flamingo Flower, Flamingo Lily, Heartflower, Flaming Flower*

Spanish: *Anturio*

Native to the tropical rain forests of Central and South America, their name derives from the Greek *'anthos'* meaning fruit and *'ouros'* meaning tail, referring to the flower structure. Anthuriums, with over 500 species, are desired for their wonderful array of leaf shapes and sizes, while others are grown for their attractive, waxy spathes that bloom all year in colourful shades of pink, red, coral, apricot and white.

Plant in partial to full shade, requires consistently moist soil, do not let dry out between waterings, will reach 12-18inches (30-45cm). Propagate by seeds, rootball division, stem or tip cuttings, rhizome cuttings and air layering. This plant is suitable for growing indoors.

Warning: The sap of this plant may cause skin irritation.

ELEPHANT EAR

Family: *Araceae*

Alocasia macrorrhiza

English: *Giant Taro, Giant Elephant Ear, Upright Elephant Ear, Pai, Giant Alocasia*

Spanish: *Alocasia, Oreja de Elephante*

The genus, Alocasia, the "*elephant ears*", has about 70 species, all indigenous to southeast Asia, from Java and Malaysia to the rainforests of India and Sri Lanka. They are closely related to Colocasia, and were formerly grouped together in a single genus as easy distinction between the two is not seen except in some DNA detail. Numerous hybrids have also been developed.

Giant taro reach impressive proportions with huge elephant ear leaves 3-6ft. (1-2m) in length and 2-4ft. (0.6-1.2m) wide. The whole plant can stand 12-15ft. (3.5-5m) tall and spread 6-10ft. (2-3m) across. It is cultivated throughout the tropics for its edible rhizomes and shoots, and are known as *'potatoes of the tropics'*.

Plant in partial to full shade, very high moisture needs, suitable for bogs and water gardens. Needs wind protection and is suitable for growing indoors. This plant is resistant to deer.

Propagate by dividing the rootball or rhizomes, tubers, corms or bulbs. The reddish seeds that develop along the spadix should be planted as soon as they ripen.

Danger: All parts of taro can cause stomach aches if ingested without cooking and proper preparation. Contact with the sap can irritatesensitive skin.

PEACE LILY

Family: *Araceae*

Spathiphyllum wallisii

English: *Peace Lily, Closet Plant*

Spanish: *Lirio de Paz*

Spaths get their name from the Greek "*spathi*" meaning "*sword*", that describes the leaves and flowers of these plants. Originally from South and Central America, mainly Colombia and Venezuela, they are today the most popular indoor plant in the U.S. and U.K., with cultivars introducing new varieties all the time.

Spaths are one of the plants used in the NASA Clean Air Study and has shown to help remove formaldehyde, benzene, and carbon monoxide from the air, making them amazing natural indoor air conditioners.

Plant in partial to full shade, requires consistently moist soil, do not let dry out between waterings, blooms all year, reaches 24-36inches (60-90cm), propagate by seed anytime or dividing the rootball in spring. Seed collecting is not recommended. Bloom repeatedly with fragrant flowers. These are the easiest houseplants to take care of.

Danger: All parts of plant are poisonous if ingested.

CORDYLINES

Family: *Agavaceae*

Genus: *Cordyline*

English: *Ti Plant, Good Luck Tree, Palm Lily, Polynesian Ti Plant, Tree of Kings*

Spanish: *Geraldina, Pabola, Caña de Indio*

Cordylines are known to the tropical world by many names and are crowned as "*King of tropical foliage*". Ti plants or cordylines, are very popular with a vast range of intense colours, leaf shapes and sizes, and are reaching high popularity among gardeners, landscapers and collectors alike.

Native from Eastern Asia to Polynesia, ti hybrids have a multitude of common names in English, French, Japanese and Hawaiian. Natives use plants for fiber, cloth and livestock food, plus medicine, perfume, varnish, and even a drink, Okolehao, in Hawaii! The roots are said to be edible. Ti is pronounced like "*tea*" in some areas, while in Florida "*tie*" is more common.

Grown for foliage, colour and mid height fillers, 4-6ft. (1-2m), they grow from a central stalk and often drop their lower leaves. Plant in partial to light shade, average water, bloom anywhere from late winter to early autumn. Propagate by air layering or cuttings. Grown for foliage.

Green & Red Ti

Hawaiian Red Ti

Green Ti Berries

I'm Blushing

Kiwi

Pele's Green

CROTONS

Family: *Euphorbiaceae*

Genus: *Codiaeum*

English: *Crotons*

Spanish: *Laurel*

Codiaeums, commonly called crotons, have at least a half dozen common names for every plant and have been enjoyed by Pacific Islanders for centuries. Crotons are native to the Moluccan Islands, between the Philippines and New Guinea. The plants were first formally studied by Dutch naturalist G.E. Rumphius and he named the plant Codiaeum—1690. In 1762, Carl von Linne applied the common name "*croton*" after the ancient Greek City, Croton.

Considered to be the world's most colourful tropical shrub, Crotons come in scores of vivid colours and dozens of leaf shapes as well. Their variable leaf colouration gives crotons their immense popularity. The yellow and green colours of the Brazilian flag are said to have originated from croton colours.

Steady growers, they branch and bush; not fussy for food, water or soil, the croton is a great tropical. Can take direct sun or shade, some grow to 15ft. (4.5m); prune as you wish for form, but basically leave this plant alone. Easily propagated or grown from seed, this plant is suitable for growing indoors, and can be used as an accent or even a nice hedge.

L. M. Rutherford

Danger: All parts of the plant are poisonous if ingested.

Tug Boat Annie

Kentucky

A. *Tartilis*

B. *General Paget*

C. *Stoplight*

D. *Duke of Windsor*

E. *Thomas Edison*

XERISCAPE GARDEN - BONAIRE, NA.

Chapter 3
Dry Environment & Xeriscaping

One of the buzz words in today's gardens is xeriscaping, pronounced: zeir-a-scaping, the word comes from two Greek words: "*xeri*" derived from "*xeros*" for dry, and "*scape*" meaning a view or scene—so "*dry scene*".

For gardeners, xeriscaping simply means landscaping with slow-growing, drought tolerant plants to conserve water, reduce yard trimmings, reduce pesticides and fertilizer use, while providing stunning shape, form, colour and attention.

Arid states along with any dry environment are suitable for xeriscaping—even tropical climates are excellent, while many plants do very well in pots and indoors so can be grown in cold climates just overwinter indoors. Besides the Americas, there is an astonishing array of drought tolerant plants native to other "Mediterranean" climates such as Southern Europe, North Africa, Western Asia, South Africa, and Australia, available to the gardener.

This chapter is designed to not only help identify the various groups of drought tolerant plants and their uses, but to give you ideas for creating your own unique and environmental friendly garden.

Remember, xeriscaping:
- Conserves water, 50% of a standard garden.
- Provides numerous planting options.
- Minimal pest and disease problems.
- Thrives with little to no fertilization.
- Low pruning and maintenance saving valuable landfill space.
- Provides amazing natural security—dry enviro plants all have either spikes, needles, thorns, serrated edges or all of the above.

ALOE - SOAP

Family: *Asphodelaceae*

Aloe saponaria syn: Aloe maculata

English: *Soap Aloe, African Aloe*

Spanish: *Aloe Jabon*

Zulu: *Icena, (plural Amacena)*

Native to South Africa, the African Aloe or Soap Aloe is so named as the sap from the juicy leaves makes suds in water and can be used as a soap substitute. Very drought and salt tolerant makes it a great choice for beachside yards to desert gardens. A stemless plant with spotted leaves and beautiful bursts of yellow, pink, orange or red flowers that attract hummingbirds.

Contrary to Aloe Vera, its sap should not be used on the skin, as it is irritating and can provoke dermatitis in sensitive people.

Plant in full sun to light shade, little to regular water, needs good drainage, propagates by offsets, clumps heavily, stalks can reach 3ft. (90cm), blooms spring through summer, reliable low-maintenance, good container plant, attractive to hummingbirds, bees and butterflies, drought-tolerant, suitable for xeriscaping.

Danger: Seed is poisonous if ingested, sap can be a skin irritant.

ALOE VERA

Family: *Asphodelaceae*

Aloe barbadensis

English: *Aloe Vera, Medicinal Aloe, Burn Plant, Barbados Aloe*

Spanish: *Acíbar, Aloe, Sábila (Mexico), Lináloe, Maguey Morado*

Aloe is a very popular genus of succulent with over 300 species occurring naturally in Africa, Madagascar, and Arabia. Thrives in climates such as the Caribbean as well as Central and South America. Aloe species vary from grass-like succulents to large trees. Aloe vera, the burn plant, is one of the first succulents ever documented. Purported to be one of the herbs Cleopatra used in her beauty regime, it has found a use in the modern era and is grown commercially for the sap which is used medicinally. These aloes, pictured, are very salt tolerant and an excellent choice for seaside gardens.

Part of the lily family aloes are sometimes confused with the agaves, but the latter (in the family Agavaceae) have fibrous leaves whereas aloe leaves are thick and juicy.

In Mexican folklore, it is said that if you cannot be successful in growing common medicinal aloe, then you are hopeless for growing any plant—try another hobby for gardening is not your thing!

Plant aloes in full sun to partial shade, natural rainfall to water or 1-2 waterings in the hot season, low maintenance, good container plants, bloom late spring into summer, suitable for xeriscaping, propagate by separating the offset pups. Can be grown indoors. Plants grown in partial shade usually look healthier and more succulent.

Danger: Handling plant may cause skin irritation or allergic reaction.

BROMELIADS

Family: *Bromeliaceae*

English: *Bromeliads, Air Plants*
Spanish: *Bromelia, Flor de Aire, Prodigiosa*

Epiphytic plants are among the most fascinating of all tropicals. Epiphytes include most orchids, many bromeliads and all stag-horn ferns. They do not require soil to grow and derive their nutrition from the air, rain water nutrients and decomposing matter.

The genus name "*Bromelia*" comes from a prominent Swedish medical doctor and botanist, Olof Ole Bromell (1639-1705). Recently evolved on the evolutionary scale they are a very diverse, highly adaptable, and one tough family of plants.

Bromeliads entered recorded history some 500 years ago when Columbus introduced the pineapple to Spain upon returning from his second voyage to the New World. On that voyage he found it being cultivated by the Caribe Indians in the West Indies.

Bromeliads are very unique, exotic looking plants whose foliage offers an extremely diversified range of sizes, colours, shapes and patterns. These include spots, scale, bands and stripes.

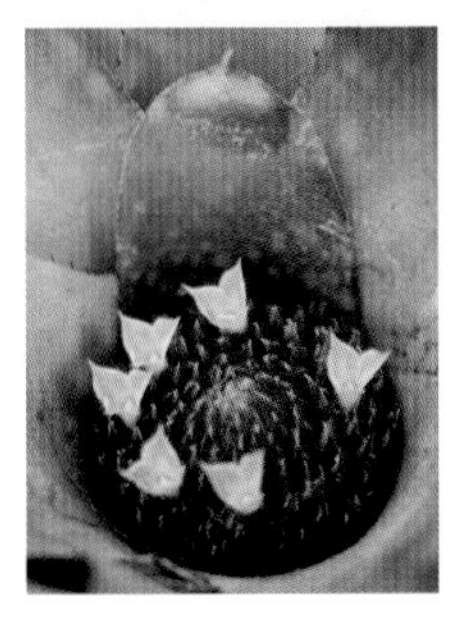

Exquisitely coloured flowers and bracts in various sizes and shapes complement these plants and last for months.

Their thick, waxy leaves form a bowl shape in the centre for catching rainwater. Some bromeliads can hold several gallons of water and are miniature ecosystems in themselves providing homes for several creatures including frogs, tadpoles, salamanders, snails, beetles, geckoes, lizards, dragon flies, ant colonies and mosquito larvae. Those that die decompose and furnish the plant with nutrients.

Because of their diversity, the Bromeliaceae family contains over 2700 described species in approximately 56 genera, research carefully before planting. Some can take desert sun, while others require partial shade to almost swamp conditions. Sizes vary greatly. Easy to grow, make good container plants, require light and ventilation, can tie to trees and palms. As the plants grow, mature, flower and pup, you can detach the pups and plant elsewhere.

One of the best kept secrets in the plant world, Bromeliads are taking their rightful place as some of the most popular plants for gardeners in temperate, subtropical and tropical regions.

Danger: All Bromeliads have sharp spiny leaf ends and most have serrated spiky edges—always wear gloves when handling, long sleeves are recommended too!

CANDLE CACTUS

Family: *Cactaceae*

Pilosocereus lanuginosus

English: *Candle Cactus, Venezuelan Columnar Cacti, Kadushi Cactus*

Spanish: *Cactus de Vela, Cacto Columnar*

Papiamento: *Kadushi*

Huge columnar cactus from northern South America and the Caribbean (Aruba, Bonaire, Curacao & Trinidad).

The candelabra shaped kadushi is a signature cacti in the ABC islands, where it's tender flesh has been used for soups, medicine and even shampoo.

The trunks are porous and after a heavy rain, can absorb so much water that the whole plant may topple over. The water-logged cactus immediately generates new sprouts from its downed trunk, as well as special "rain roots" to catch every drop. The dead cacti will dry out and present a very lightweight wood.

Note: These species depend strictly on nectar-feeding bats for their pollination, a process that enhances levels of genetic diversity within their populations.

Plant in full sun, nature water, will reach 30ft.(9m), drought-tolerant, suitable for xeriscaping. Propagate from seeds in early spring, cuttings in summer. Blooms open at night and last a day. Fruit and flowers appear in the dry season when most other plants are dormant

Danger: Plant has lots of sharp spines, use extreme caution when handling.

English: *Agave, Century Plant, American Aloe, Maguey*

Spanish: *Planta de Siglo, Agave*

CENTURY PLANT

Family: *Agavaceae*

Agave americana

This desert native of Mexico, along with it's agave brethren and cultivars (over 400), are considered amazing multi-use plants. From impermeable fencing in Mexico and Central America to sweet roasted stalks, bread flour, soup thickener, first aid, rope, alcohol, and herbal medicinal remedies for indigestion to jaundice—agaves do it all.

Sisal and henequen are fibrous ropes made from the leaves of *Agave sisalana* and *Agave fourcroydes*.

Pulque is a beer-like drink made from the fermented sap of *Agave salmiana*. Tequila is distilled from the sap of blue agave (*A. tequilana*) and mescal is made by distilling fire-roasted agave, and is often sold with a worm (actually the caterpillar of the agave moth) in the bottle.

Century plants have no stem, but thick massive leaves originate from a basal rosette. They do not actually take a century to bloom; about 6-10 years in warm climates, up to 60 years in colder, then a spectacular branched flower stalk shoots up 20-40ft. (6-12m) bearing clusters of bright yellow flowers. After flowering the whole thing dies leaving dozens of pups over it's lifetime to grow anew.

Plant in full sun, can take lousy soil, water only in the summer, grow well in pots, drought tolerant, propagate by offsets and seed. The plant will reach 4-6ft. (1.2-1.8m) in height and width, and even larger, so spacing is critical when designing with these plants.

Danger: Plant has needle sharp spines use extreme caution when handling. The sap can cause a severe rash to burn/blister on bare skin. Do not attempt homemade brews or medicinal concoctions.

MINI CENTURY PLANT

Family: *Cactaceae*

Agave gypsophila

CROWN OF THORNS

Family: *Euphorbiaceae*

Euphorbia milii

English: *Crown of Thorns, Christ Plant, Christ Thorn, Siamese Lucky Plant*

Spanish: *la Corona de Jesucristo*

Named after the ancient Greek physician, Euphorbus, and Baron Milius, who introduced the species into cultivation in France in 1821.

From Madagascar, this woody semi-succulent is popularly believed to be the thorn used during Christ's crucifixion. Very popular in Asia, where it is believed to bring good luck, there are an amazing number of hybrids and cultivars including dwarf varieties.

The "flowers", in red through yellow, are in actual fact showy bracts, which bloom freely throughout the year.

Plant in sun to partial shade, average water (do not overwater), suitable for growing indoors, needs little maintenance, propagate from stem cuttings or seed, will reach 24-36inches (60-90cm). Makes an excellent natural security barrier.

Danger: As with the other Euphorbias, its sap, or latex, is poisonous if ingested in large amounts, it irritates the skin like poison ivy, and can cause temporary blindness if it goes in the eyes. The latex also contributes to the protection of the plants from herbivores and has been used as arrow poison. Do not plant near fish stocked pools or ponds.

DESERT ROSE

Family: *Apocynaceae*

Adenium obesum

English: *Desert Rose*
Spanish: *Rosa de Desierto*

One of the most popular plants in the world, this native from east Africa will reach 4-6ft. (1.2-1.8m), but has been observed twice that height in the wild, with huge funnel shaped trunks. The "*obesum*" name refers to the large fat base of the plant. It blooms from spring through autumn with an array of fantastic flowers in shades of pink, rose, white or red.

Plant in full sun, average water, to avoid rot do not water in dormant stage which is signaled by the dropping of all leaves and blooms. Can be propagated by woody stem cuttings, only seedlings will develop the coveted bulbous base. Suitable for bonsai.

Excellent pot plant, great indoors, always at its best with some attention, will become larger, more interesting and more valuable every year.

Danger: Parts of this plant are poisonous if ingested.

English: *Florida Bromeliad*
Spanish: *Bromelia, Flor de Aire*

FLORIDA BROMELIAD

Family: *Bromeliaceae*

Tillandsi fasciculata

There are approximately 16 species of Florida Bromeliads and are distinct from the West Indian populations from which they originated. There is also genetic variation among populations of certain species within the state.

All of Florida's native species of bromeliads are epiphytic, although some species may sometimes be found growing terrestrially.

GIANT MILKWEED

Family: *Asclepiadaceae*

Calotropis procera

English: *Rubber Bush, Apple of Sodom, Giant Milkweed*

Spanish: *Mala Hierba de Leche Gigante*

This African milkweed species is widely distributed throughout the Caribbean and is often an indicator of overgrazed land or habitats degraded first by sugar cane cultivation and then by cattle and goats.

A magnificent shrub, reaching 10ft. (3m) with large silver-green leaves, clusters of waxy purple-tipped flowers, and inflated green seed pods. The pods split open when ripe to release silk-tufted seed to the wind.

Calotrope is commonly harvested for its medicinal properties, the acrid sap latex is used to treat infected wounds and skin problems in people, and to treat parasitic skin infestations in animals. It also yields ash for making gunpowder, and an extremely strong fibre.

Plant in full sun, salt and drought tolerant, blooms all year, propagate from woody stem cuttings. Highly attractive to Monarch butterflies. May be considered a noxious weed or invasive.

Danger: Parts of plant are poisonous if ingested, the latex is poisonous, containing digitalis-like compounds that affect the heart, and is used to make arrow poison.

Handling plant may cause skin irritation or allergic reaction.

English: *Heart of Flame, False Pineapple*
Spanish: *Piña de Falso*

HEART OF FLAME

Family: *Bromeliaceae*

Bromelia balansae

From South America another effective security plant for natural barriers, reaching heights of 2-3ft. (60-90cm) but will spread leaves to 6ft. (1.8m) and form impenetrable thickets.

Watch for leaves gradually changing from a shiny green to a reddish colour which will indicate the start of an amazing flowering. A spectacular flower rosette is produced on a dense panicle that arises from the heart of the plant.

Plant in full sun to partial shade, tough, drought-tolerant, suitable for xeriscaping, average water, naturally reproduces vegetatively by means of thick runners just underground. It is usually propagated by separating the runner plants—very fast grower; proliferous. Space 3-4ft. (90-120cm).

Danger: Plant leaves are serrated and armed with sharp, recurved prickles, use extreme caution, thick gloves and long sleeves when handling.

MANDACARU

Family: *Cactaceae*

Cereus jamacaru

English: *Pleated Cereus, Mandacaru, Nagblom, Queen of the Night*

Spanish: *Mandacaru, Reina de la Noche*

The name of this Genus is derived from the Greek "*cereus*" for wax. Originally from Brazil and first described in 1768, these cacti have undergone multiple culivations so that positive identification is almost impossible. Now found throughout the islands and Florida they have the classic cereus flower.

Plant in full sun, drought-tolerant, suitable for xeriscaping, will reach 30ft. (9m) in height, segmented stems. Flowers, in big batches throughout the summer. Propagation: seeds in spring, cuttings in summer.

Danger: Plant has very sharp spines so use extreme caution when handling.

MELON CACTUS

Family: *Cactaceae*

Melocactus macracanthos

English: *Melon Cactus, Fez Cactus, Turk's Cap*
Spanish: *Cactus de Melón*
Papiamento: *Milon di Seru - (melon of the hills)*

One of the true natives of the Caribbean, Melon Cactus originates from Curacao. Mature specimens develop a crown named cephalium and the thorns, like all cacti, are modified leaves. A self pollinating genus, flowers are pink tubes that pop out from the red cephalium on top of the plant. Will reach no more than 6-12inches (15-30cm) when fully grown.

Melocacti are very popular and under intense survival pressure as people collect them in their native habitats only to discover they die when transplanted. Purchase and cultivate Melocacti only from seed.

Plant in full sun, well drained soil, regular water in summer, much less in winter, needs a greenhouse or indoors for frost conditions, propagate from seed, germinate in vitro in gelatin, agar or other medium. Drought-tolerant, suitable for xeriscaping.

Danger: Plant has hard sharp spines use extreme caution when handling. Some species are protected and you can be charged if found in your possession.

NIGHT BLOOMING CACTUS

Family: *Cactaceae*

Hylocereus undatus

English: *Red Pitaya, Strawberry Pear, Night-blooming Cereus, Queen of the Night, Honolulu Queen, Belle of the Night, Cinderella Plant*

Spanish: *Flor de Cáliz, Reina de la Noche, Chacam, Chak-Wob, Junco Tapatio, Pitahaya, Pitahaya Orejona, Tasajo, Zacamb*

A vine climbing cactus that can reach over 40ft. (12m) found throughout the American tropics. Of unknown origin, this night-blooming cactus resembles nothing more than a dead bush most of the year, but each summer, its exquisitely scented flowers open at nightfall, then close forever with the heat of the morning sun—a lovely flower presented to the world for a fleeting glimpse. They have a tuberous, turnip-like root usually weighing 5-15lb (2.25-6.75kg) which Native Americans used as a food source.

Plant in full sun to partial shade, regular water, blooms late spring to early autumn, fragrant flowers, suitable for indoors, propagate from semi-hardwood cuttings.

English: *Pineapple*
Spanish: *Piña*

PINEAPPLE

Family: *Bromeliaceae*

Anana comosus

The most notable of the Bromeliaceae family and developed commercially by man is the edible pineapple. Native to Tropical America, it had been cultivated by native Americans for several centuries before the arrival of Europeans. In fact, a pineapple seed is one of the rarest things in the world as the natives constantly chose seedless plants, (easy to eat), to recultivate in their own genetic improvement of the species.

A rosette plant in colours of red, blues, purples and silver/greys, it takes 2 years to mature enough to bloom and produce fruit.

Plant in full sun to partial shade, will reach 24-36inches (60-90cm), blooms spring into summer, normal water, let dry between waterings, likes fertilizer, suitable for growing indoors.

Easy to grow by cutting the leafy top from a commercial pineapple, allow to dry 1-2 weeks. Root in moist medium that drains well. Water once a week until roots appear, transfer to a one gallon (4 litre) pot for growing.

Can also propagate by division or from herbaceous stem cuttings. Research the methods and procedures for seed collecting and cultivation.

Danger: Parts of plant are poisonous if ingested, leaves have sawtooth edges.

There are a host of cultivars that can be divided into two main groups:

A: CAYENNE – Most of the varieties of Pineapple sold in the international market belong to this group.

A1: SMOOTH CAYENNE – from Central & West Africa, distinguished by their yellow/orange colour are sold worldwide.

A2: CHAMPAKA – from Central America, distinguished by their dark green external colouration when ripe, and are sold in the northern markets of the European Union.

A3: MD2 – from Central America and also known as EXTRA SWEET, they are distinguished by low acidity, a deep orange external colouration and yellow flesh.

B: QUEEN – Grown in South Africa, Zimbabwe, Kenya, Mauritius and the Reunion Islands, the VICTORIA variety belonging to this group, is a smaller fruit with a delicate flavor and is targeted mainly for a top-of-the-range niche market.

English: *Prickly Pear, Prickly Pear Cactus, Palma-Brava, Opúntia*

Spanish: *Nopal, Chumbera de Puas, Tuna Brava, Higo de Mar*

PRICKLY PEAR - Magenta

Family: *Cactaceae*

Opuntia cochenillifera

There are over 200 species of prickly pear cacti, most are found in southwestern North America, Mexico, Central America and South America. The sweet juicy fruits of the prickly pear, called tunas, are very popular everywhere except the United States. In fact, annual worldwide commercial production of prickly pear tunas is more than twice that of strawberries, avocados, or apricots! The pads, called nopales, are a popular vegetable in Mexico and Central America. They are usually cooked but can be eaten raw. They taste a little like green beans. The fruit can also be made into preserves or syrup—has a watermelon flavour. However their fragrant flowers, great colours and natural barrier abilities make them very popular in gardens.

MAGENTA PRICKLY PEAR
Opuntia cochenillifera

Prickly pear is easy to grow, rooting readily from pads stuck in the ground, or even just lying on the surface. Plant in full sun, will reach 4-8ft. (1.2-2.4m) in height and spread, blooms late spring through summer, drought tolerant, suitable for xeriscaping, average to rainfall only for water, suitable for growing indoors and in pots, propagate from seed or by rooting a pad, attractive to bees, hummingbirds and bats.

NOTE: In some areas these plants may be considered a protected species; check before digging or gathering seeds.

Danger: Handling plant may cause skin irritation, puncture wounds and/or allergic reaction—use extreme caution and protection when handling.

PRICKLY PEAR - Yellow

Family: *Cactaceae*

Opuntia monacantha

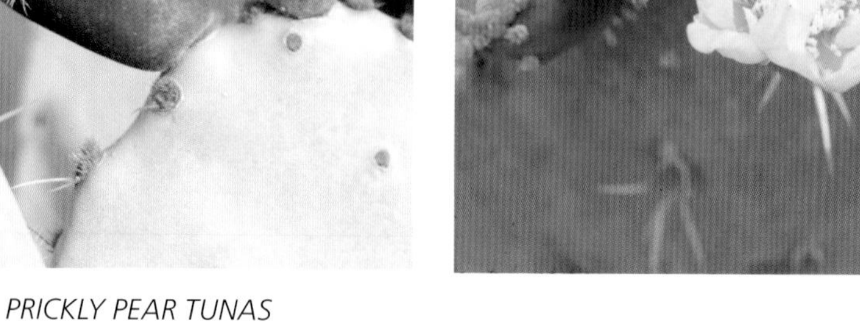

PRICKLY PEAR TUNAS

English: *Spanish Bayonet, Dagger Plant, Aloe Yucca*

Spanish: *Bayoneta de Española*

SPANISH BAYONET

Family: *Agavaceae*

Yucca aloifolia

This coastal native from North Carolina to Mexico and including all the West Indies is considered the ultimate in security plants. Can be planted as a wild fence, along a fence line, under windows or around anything needing a natural barrier. There are several species and cultivars and are known for their hardiness, fabulous spires of flowers, and ability to thicket grow.

Plant in full sun to partial shade, drought-tolerant, suitable for xeriscaping, will reach 8-20ft. (2.4-6m), blooms anytime from late spring to early autumn. Propagate by seeds, root cuttings, and offsets. You can actually cut a branch off with a hand saw and shove into a hole in the ground, water, and it will grow.

Danger: Has hypodermic needle sharp spines, use extreme caution when handling, can inflict painful puncture wounds even through heavy clothing! Wear thick gloves.

SPANISH MOSS

Family: *Bromeliaceae*

Tillandsia usneoides

English: *Spanish Moss, Florida Moss, Long Moss, Graybeard*

Spanish: *Barba de Viejo, Musgo de Espanola*

Actually, Spanish Moss is neither Spanish nor a moss, but an epiphytic plant which grows on another plant, does not have any roots, and uses its long, thin, scaly stems to wrap around the host tree and hang down from the branches. The leaves are covered with cup-like, permeable scales that "catch" moisture and nutrients from the air.

Believed to be from the Peruvian Andes and now native in coastal areas from Virginia south to Argentina and Chile, it has the broadest natural geographic range of any bromeliad.

Spanish moss was harvested for years as a stuffing material in automobile seats, furniture, and mattresses. Moss pickers were hired and used long poles to pull the stringy masses off the trees. The plants were then dried and cured before being used.

Long, thick masses may reach 20ft. (6m) in length. Prefers moisture and partial shade but can withstand long dry periods, suitable for xeriscaping, have very tiny seeds and inconspicuous flowers that bloom late spring early summer.

Propagation: small fragments and seeds are dispersed by wind and birds that easily reproduce new plants. To start your own collection just ask a friend for some, take some down from a tree, pick it up off the ground after a big wind, purchase at your local garden centre, or order online.

ALPINIA GINGERS – SOUTH FLORIDA

Chapter 4
Gingers

These wonderful and exotic gems are incredibly diverse in all aspects, from origin to variety of species, colours, designs and sizes. Their amazing to outrageous designs make them a favorite in the home and garden, cut flower markets, hotels and resorts, as well as subjects for designers, photographers, painters and other artists.

Gingers are wonderful garden plants for the Southern United States and all parts of the world with warm humid climates. They are quite hardy and easy to grow. Many can also be grown in pots, overwintered indoors, or grown in conservatories. But it's their delicate and astonishingly fragrant scents that have made them popular worldwide.

There are nine basic groups of gingers, six groups are represented with some of the more common tropical garden varieties shown.

ALPINIAS

Family: *Zingiberaceae*

Genus: *Alpinia*

The scent of the lance-like leaves when brushed up against is an unforgettable spicy bouquet of ginger. Alpinia have different pubesens, waxy cascading shell like flowers or soft cerise bracts of reds and pinks or even cone-shaped. Whichever you prefer, the leaves have that wonderful aroma. Easy to grow requiring well draining soil kept on the moist side and preferring humidity and partial sun/shade. Some varieties will not tolerate periods of cold and should be removed for winter storage. They make very impressive container plants or can be planted in the garden forming wonderful hedges and fillers.

Regular, miniature, dwarf, and variegated species.

RED CONE GINGER PLANT
Alpinia purpurata

English: *Red Ginger, Red Cone Ginger, Ostrich Plume Ginger*

Spanish: *Alpinia, Jengibre de Rojo*

A native of Malaya, this very popular ginger is composed of layers of red cerise bracts; the actual flower is a miniature whitish bloom that appears behind the bracts. Frequently used in the cut flower industry, huge "blooms" can be 8 inches (20cm) long, last up to three weeks on the plant and will produce plantlets as the flower begins to fade. Blooms most of the year. Does best in full sun to part shade. Blooms at 3-4ft. (90-120cm); and can grow to 8-9ft. (1.5-2m). Makes an excellent potted plant.

PINK CONE GINGER PLANT
Alpinia purpurata

SHELL GINGER
Alpinia zerumbet

English: *Shell Ginger, Cone Ginger*

Spanish: *Alpinia, Jengibre de Concha*

From China, shell gingers give you that tropical look in solid blocks of green foliage and fragrant flower clusters. This Alpinia puts out large arching sprays of fragrant, long lasting, waxy flowers, resembling white sea shells, which open to reveal a vivid orange interior. Foliage comes in greens or variegated form. Herbal medicine derived from the ground leaves is sold as anti-hypertension and anti-stress medication.

Often listed as a naturalized species in Hawaii and Florida, they make excellent landscape subjects.

Plant in full sun to partial shade, moderately rich soil, grows quickly, can reach 10-12ft. (3-3.6m). Will tolerate some drought and frost, has large pendant inflorescence with white and pink flowers, blooms all year round but especially in spring, Has multiple synonyms. Very similar species: Alpinia henryi.

COSTUS – SPIRAL GINGERS

Family: *Costaceae*

Genus: *Costus*

Costus is the wonderful world of spiral ginger, and are easily distinguished from other commonly cultivated gingers because the leaves spiral around the main stem. Some varieties have a velvety soft texture on the backs of its leaves, while others may be smooth with purple undersides. The Costus species is rich and varied in form, flower and growing conditions. Its bracts and flowers can range from a cone-like bract to pineapple-shaped or soft, ruffled flowers emerging from cones. Colours from white to bright orange. There are short mounding, spreading, and upright forms. Heights range from 1-10ft.+ (30cm-3m). Like Alpinias they are very easy to grow, do well in partial sun in mild climates and partial shade in hot climates. They love a rich, well draining soil kept on the moist side. They make beautiful garden specimens or container plants.

Crepe gingers are a very attractive costus from Asia. Clustering reed-like stems 8-10ft. (2.5-3m) in height.

Three inch (7.5cm) ruffled fringed round white petals appear three or four at a time from a glossy red terminal cone, which stays red till the flower is finished. Blooms mid-summer to autumn. Can take partial sun to full shade.

CREPE GINGER
Costus speciosus

English: *Crepe Ginger, Malay Ginger*

Spanish: *Jengibre de Crepe*

RED TOWER GINGER
Costus barbatus

English: *Red Tower Ginger, Spiral Ginger, Red Velvet Ginger*

Spanish: *Cana de Jabali, Apagafuego, Sangrafu*

A native of Costa Rica, this costus is a very popular cut flower which can last as long as a month on the plant. The large inflorescence is comprised of a series of hard red bracts similar to a pine-apple cone shape with small bright yellow flowers peeking out. Grows 6-8ft. (2-2.5m), can take full sun, blooms spring through summer, makes a handsome landscape or tub subject.

TROPICAL GINGER
Costus pulverulentus

English: *Tropical Ginger, Spiral Ginger*
Spanish: *Jengibre de Tropical*

Costus pulverulentus—a large Costus from Central and South America. Because of variable appearance, is sometimes confused with *Costus spicatus*. Interestingly, scientists feel this species, although variable in appearance, seems to be completely specialized on the long-tailed hermit hummingbird (*Phaethornis superciliosus*) for pollination across its range. It makes a fabulous shrub filler, grows to 6ft. (2m) in height, fills out constantly, prefers partial to full shade, moist soil, is an evergreen with constant blooming red-orange flowering bracts.

HIDDEN GINGER - Hybrid

CURCUMA

Family: *Zingiberaceae*

Genus: *Curcuma*

Curcumas are the world of hidden gingers, which get their name from flowers on short stalks hidden amid their foliage.

Plant in light shade and moist soil, will reach to 4ft. (1.2m), average water, spring fertilize, blooms appear spring through autumn depending on variety. Most varieties are very hardy, but go dormant for the winter where they will die down to rest. Keep on the dry side while resting for the winter.

Propagate by division or seed. For seed collecting, allow pods to dry on plant then break open to collect seeds.

This amazing and beautiful ginger has wide corrugated banana like leaves that open up to an inflorescent cream spire bract with a lavender pink rim up to a spectacular lavender/pink crown. It is very pest-free, spectacular massed and is a great foliage plant.

PASTEL HIDDEN GINGER

Curcuma cordata

English: *Jewel of Thailand, Hidden Ginger*

Spanish: *Jengibre de Escondido*

TORCH GINGER

Family: *Zingiberaceae*

Genus: *Etlingera*

Etlingeras are outrageous gingers with huge, royal scepter-like flowers in red, pink, rose, gold and white. They bloom atop tall stalks and the plant reaches 12-17ft. (4-6m) in height. There is also a dwarf variety available. Very exotic, they hail from the far east and Asia. Require partial sun to full shade, are attractive to bees, butterflies and birds, require consistently moist soil. The flowers are excellent for cutting and display.

RED TORCH GINGER

Etlingera elatior

English: *Red Torch Ginger*

Spanish: *Bastion de Emperador O Torcha, Antorcha de Rojo, Lirio Antorcha, Boca de Dragón*

Its inflorescence comes out of the ground instead of the terminal spike, thus making it easier to cut as a cut flower. The bracts are cherry red with yellow edges. As the bract opens up the lower bract leaves turn down revealing a spectacular cone shaped torch. An exceptional ginger for the garden or greenhouse, needs a warm climate or greenhouse.

HEDYCHIUMS

Family: *Zingiberaceae*

Genus: *Hedychium*

Hedychiums, around 50 species, make fabulous tropical subjects for the garden. From Asia, they are known commonly as the ginger lilies and fill the air with breathtaking fragrances from their blooms. The genus name derives from two ancient Greek words, "*hedys*" meaning sweet and "*chios*" meaning "snow". The correct pronunciation is head-dick-e-um!

Hedychiums come in a huge range of colours. Showy butterfly shaped blooms emerge from the terminal spike atop a cane like growth. Grow to 4-6ft. (1.2-2m) in height, in any good garden soil or potted container. Prefer light shade and moist soil. Bloom late spring through autumn. Hedychiums are more cold hardy than most gingers, and often called Hardy Ginger Lily. Propagate by dividing rhizomes, tubers, corms or bulbs (including offsets). Their popularity with growers increases and *Hedychium gardnerianum* (Kahili Ginger) is often used in cross hybridizing to make new varieties.

CULTIVAR - Anne S. Bishop

This hybrid, cultivated by Anne, likes sun to partial shade, will grow 6-8ft. (1.8-2.4 m), making it a great backdrop filler. Large golden yellow flowers, a darker yellow throat and orange red stamen adorn this tall open spike of inflorescence. Very sweet tropical fragrance. Blooms summer through autumn.

WHITE BUTTERFLY GINGER
Hedychium coronarium

English: *White Ginger, Garland Lily, Butterfly Ginger*

Spanish: *Jengibre de Mariposa*

Each individual flower on the terminal green cone looks like a white butterfly in flight. One whiff of the highly perfumed flower conjures up mental images of romantic, moonlit tropical nights.

Likes rich soil with adequate moisture. Needs some sun to bloom and shade to grow up to 6ft. (2m). It makes a nice background plant and looks great planted in large clumps in a woodsy area. Often can be seen growing wild alongside the road and creek banks. Plant it near a patio, porch, deck or window so you can enjoy their amazing fragrance.

Originally from Asia, Himalayan, this outrageous ginger will reach 4-6ft. (1.2-1.8m) with close ranks of waxy leaves, its spike features six precise rows of small orange flowers with 3 inch orange stamens projecting outwards. Grows best when protected from mid-day sun, moist soil, hardy, blooms summer through autumn, very fragrant, very popular.

ORANGE BOTTLEBRUSH GINGER

Hedychium coccineum

English: *Red Butterfly Ginger, Orange Bottlebrush Ginger*

Spanish: *Jengibre de Botella-cepillar*

ZINGIBERS

Family: *Zingiberaceae*

Genus: *Zingiber*

Zingibers are native to tropical Asia—the spice islands—have highly aromatic leaves and rhizomes, are used to flavour meats and fish, make medicines and even shampoo, with one species producing edible ginger used in cooking.

Zingibers are an easy to grow member of the ginger family, they love heat and humidity but prefer the shade of filtered sun. Bloom from summer through autumn. Propagate by division, stem cuttings and seeds. Very attractive in the garden and as a cut flower.

GOLDEN BEEHIVE GINGER
Zingiber spectabile

English: *Black Gingerwort, Golden Beehive Ginger*

Spanish: *Micrófono*

Truly spectacular as the name implies Golden Beehive Ginger, a native to Malaysia, will reach 6-8ft. (2-2.6m), and will present you with the most unique flower bracts with an incredible honeycomb construction. The bracts are pale yellow in a young inflorescence, becoming red as it matures, especially if it gets some full sun. Small purple flowers will emerge between bracts, all parts of this plant have a strong gingery fragrance.

English: *Heliconia—derived from Mt.Helicon in Greece*

Spanish: *Barco de Caridad, Platano Cimarron, Platanio O Bijao*

Other Common Names: lobster claw, wild plantain, flowering banana, parrot's flower, macaw flower, false bird-of-paradise.

HELICONIAS

Family: *Heliconiaceae*

Genus: *Heliconia*

HELICONIA GARDEN – SOUTH FLORIDA

Heliconia are related to plants such as bananas and the Traveler's tree, and are often referred to as "*designer bananas*". Grown for their beautiful, brilliant, colourful flowering bracts, these breathtaking and unusual designs may be erect, pendulous or spiraling with bracts in the shapes of bird's beaks, lobster claws or fan shaped. They are enormously popular in the cut flower industry.

Native to Northern South America, Central America and the West Indies, there are at least 200-250 named varieties.

Common names for Heliconias abound, none of which are meaningful to identify a specific variety. What you see in the photos is the Heliconia's waxy bract that produces vivid colours and exotic complex tropical shapes, the real flowers are fairly inconspicuous inside the colourful sheaths. The most common bract colours are reds, yellows and oranges, while some types are grown only for their colourful leaves. Stem and leaf growth is always vertical with leaves pointed up.

Heliconias vary greatly in plant size, from a low at about 2ft. (60cm), while others reach10ft. (3m) or more. Most are between at 4-6ft. (1.2-1.8m), and bloom spring through autumn, and require consistently moist soil.

Some Heliconia are an excellent choice for container plants that can be grown indoors for the winter and moved outdoors for the spring and summer.

STEM HELICONIA

LOBSTER CLAW - Red
Heliconia caribaea

LOBSTER CLAW
Heliconia orthotricha

LOBSTER CLAW - Yellow
Heliconia wagneriana

RED / YELLOW GYRO
Heliconia lathispatha

ORANGE FLAME
Heliconia caribaea

GOLDEN TORCH
Heliconia spathocircinata

PENDENT HELICONIA

PERU
Heliconia rostrata

FLYING BIRD
Heliconia trichocarpa

DAY LILY GARDEN – SOUTH GEORGIA

Chapter 6
Lilies

Welcome to the colourful and immensely popular world of lilies whose history dates back to at least ancient Minoan times—the very beginning of western culture.

Originating from all over the world, exotics, imports, hybrids by the thousands, plus ponds and aquatics are now available.

Societies, clubs, meets, shows, growers, and specialty nurseries are everywhere and the millions of websites on the internet have all the information you would ever want and every bulb for sale too.

Lily varieties are endless and include Asiatics, Orientals, L.A. Hybrids, Tiger Lilies, Trumpets, and Daylilies. Some like Daylilies are not true lilies —true lilies belong in the genus Lilium, grow from bulbs, have stiff stems, narrow strap like leaves, and large showy flowers.

These flowers may be trumpet, bowl, or bell shaped with reflexed petals, face downward, up, or out, come in a huge variety of colours, and are often wonderfully fragrant.

Read up and do a little research on bulbs, planting and care, visit nurseries and formal gardens when lilies are in bloom to get ideas and see colours. Hardy, minimal care, lilies bring height, fragrance, and great colour to any summer garden.

AMARYLLIS

Family: *Amaryllidaceae*

Genus: *Hippeastrum*

English: *Amaryllis, Barbados Lily*
Spanish: *Tararaco, Azucena de Méjico*

Between 1930 and 1954 there occurred probably the best-known dispute on the application of a plant name as two groups of scientists and botanists, using information and arguments from as far back as the 1700's, went at it over Hippeastrum versus Amaryllis for a genus name. Fortunately *we* do not have to fuss except to decide over which astonishing array of colours and cultivars to choose for our gardens.

From South America and possibly the Caribbean, Ams are hugely popular with at least 50 varieties being grown commercially and umpteen cultivars having great names like Naked Lady and Pink Floyd!

Plant in full sun to partial shade, average water, will reach at least 18-24 inches (45-60cm), bloom mid summer into mid-autumn, propagate by seed or dividing bulbs. Seed collecting, allow pods to dry on plant then break open to collect seeds. Note: seeds do not store well, sow as soon as possible. Fragrant flowers, are attractive to bees and butterflies, suitable for growing indoors year round. Deer resistant and make great cut flowers.

Note: winter bulb storage and treatment is very important to ensure a good and rich flowering —advise some additional research before growing.

Danger: Parts of these plants are poisonous if ingested.

CANNA LILY

Family: *Cannaceae*

Canna indica

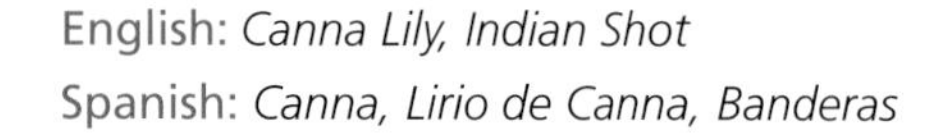
English: *Canna Lily, Indian Shot*
Spanish: *Canna, Lirio de Canna, Banderas*

Native to the tropical New World, Central and South America, these beautiful plants are associated with the Victorian era, whence they were very popular. From the Greek, for a type of reed, Canna are very hardy and easy to grow, provide big, bold splashes of colour with large, tropical appearing foliage that itself can be variegated blue-greens to burgundy, black and bronze.

Plant in full sun, in rich, fertile soil, will range from 30 inches (76cm) to more than 8ft. (2.4 m) in height, bloom repeatedly late spring through mid-autumn. Requires consistently moist soil, do not let dry out between waterings. Attractive to bees and butterflies, do well in large pots or tubs. Propagate by dividing bulbs in the spring or from seed, direct sow after last winter frost.

Seed collecting, allow seedheads to dry on plants then remove and collect seeds. Properly cleaned, the seeds can be successfully stored. The dried hard seeds are used in jewelry and cherished by African musicians for their use in shakers, and were even used in shot, hence Indian Shot, for old muzzle loading rifles.

There are hundreds of named cultivars, with their spectacular flowers being the main reason Cannas are so highly prized. Plant in masses with bananas, gingers and palms for a bold and enormous tropical foliage statement in the garden.

English: *Cape Lily, Powell's Crinum Lily*
Spanish: *Lirio de Cape, Tararaco*
Zulu: *Umnduze*

CAPE LILY

Family: *Amaryllidaceae*

Crinum X powellii

In the 19th century, English plant breeders crossed two species of South African crinum lilies, *C. bulbispermum* and *C. moorei*, to create the hybrid *Crinum X powellii*, or Cape lily. The Cape lily has gone on to become one of the most popular perennials ever.

Many garden crinums, the "*milk and wine lilies*", have striped flowers, but Cape Lily has flowers that are either all white or all pink. Most cultivars are some shade of pink.

The crinum lilies are similar to spider lilies (*Hymenocallis*) and amaryllises (*Amaryllis*), but can be distinguished by having basal rosettes of whorled leaves, unlike those of the others which have their leaves in two distinct ranks. There are some 130 species in the genus Crinum, with only a few species cultivated but hundreds of hybrids.

Easy to grow, low maintenance, whether cared for or not, the incredible Cape lily creates copious quantities of big beautiful blossoms all summer long. Plant in full sun to partial shade, regular water, propagate by dividing bulbs every 3-5 years. Good indoor plant, make nice cut flowers.

Danger: All parts of these plants are poisonous if ingested and the sap may cause skin eruptions.

CRINUM LILLIES

Family: *Amaryllidaceae*

Genus: *Crinum*

English: *Crinum Lily, Sumatra Lily, Spider Lily, Milk-and-Wine Lily, Queen Emma*

Spanish: *Lirio de Cinta*

GIANT SPIDER LILY
Crinum amabile

Native to tropical and subtropical Asia, some also come from South Africa, the Middle East and Florida, Crinum lilies make an imposing presence in the garden. A hardy giant, evergreen, member of the amaryllis family, producing large clusters of fragrant flowers in the warm season, is now a favorite landscape plant in Florida and other warm climate areas. They are pollinated at night by the amazing hawk moth with it's 4inch (10cm) proboscis.

Low maintenance, easy to grow, plant in direct sun to partial shade, adaptable to many conditions, the crinum will grow best if it dries between waterings. Likes water, mulch and fertilizer, will reach 3-5ft.+ (90-150cm), fragrant flowers, bloom spring through autumn. Good cut flower.

To propagate crinums, dig up a clump and separate the small offset bulbs from the parent bulb. Plant these in pots or directly in the garden where they will quickly root to form new plants. Watchout bulbs can reach 25lbs. (11kilos)!

GRAND CRINUM
Crinum asiaticum

THE DAY LILIES

Family: *Liliaceae*

Genus: *Hemerocallis*

English: *Day Lilies, Day Beauty*
Spanish: *Lirio de Dia, Preciosidad de Dia*

The beautiful Daylily originated in the temperate parts of Asia—Japan, Korea, Siberia, and China. Hemerocallis, from the Greek "*hemera*" (day) and "*kallos*" (beauty). Not a true lily as it roots rather than has bulbs, about 20 original species are known but cultivars have created so many variations that there are quite literally hundreds of named varieties, and have largely replaced the true species.

Hybridizers in the United States and England, working since the 1930's, have created hundreds of colours, blossom designs and sizes. Not to mention fabulous names like: Daylily A Go Go, A Kiss for Kathy, A Bauble For Bilbo, A La Mode and my personal favorite, A Moose Fishing On A Pond On Monday!

Easy to grow in most any soil, plant in full sun to partial shade, bright colours like sun to snap while dark colours will reach full colour saturation in some shade.

Average water (do not over water), will reach heights of up to 4ft. (1.2m), although 12-20inches (30-50cm) is more common, blooms spring through summer, propagate by division, grassy foliage, easy to transplant. Most varieties bloom only briefly (one day per flower), but hybrids can carry 20-30 buds per stalk. Very popular, nice and happy.

English: *Lily of the Nile, African Lily*
Spanish: *Lirio de el Nilo*
Zulu: *Ubani, (plural Izimbani)*

LILY OF THE NILE

Family: *Liliaceae*

Agapanthus africanus

From South Africa, collected and described as early as 1679, these very popular and great looking lilies have several varieties including dwarfs. Hardy, naturalize easily, gardeners love them for their ease of growth as Agapanthus make good background plants, hi-light trees and beds, or as edging along a fence, driveway, or wall.

Plant in full sun, average water, will reach 24-36inches (60-90cm), blooms late spring through early autumn, propagate by dividing bulbs in early spring, easy to start from seed, but may take up to 3 years to bloom from seed. Nicely fragrant, attractive to bees and butterflies, good container plants, make nice cut flowers, winter indoors if freezing occurs.

Danger: Handling plant may cause skin irritation or allergic reaction.

RED HOT POKER

Family: *Asphodelaceae*

Kniphofia caulescens

English: *Red Hot Poker, Torch Lily*

Spanish: *Lirio de Antorcha*

Zulu: *Icacane, (plural Amacacane)*

There are about 70 species and numerous cultivars in the torch lily line. Native to southern and eastern Africa, red hot pokers are a real eye-catcher! Both evergreen and deciduous they are a bee favorite. Colours will range from red-orange, yellow, half and half, with pink, mauve and green cultivars—with miniature pistils emerging from the bottom of each flower stem. Easy to grow, great backdrop in flower beds, or boldly up front—for something zippy in your garden red hot pokes are it.

Plant in full sun to partial shade, average water, water well in flowering season, will reach 4-6ft. (1.2-1.8m), blooms mid summer through into autumn, propagate by dividing the rootball. Large clumps can be lifted and divided, using a spade and then replanted. Drought-tolerant, suitable for xeriscaping. Deer resistant.

English: *Hurricane Lily, Red Spider Lily*
Spanish: *Lirio de Rojo Cinta*

RED SPIDER LILY

Family: *Liliaceae*

Lycoris radiata

Native to China and Japan, and now widely naturalized in the southeastern United States, spider lilies are very popular. Seemingly overnight and out of nowhere, clusters of brilliant red flowers appear out of the ground.

There are several similar species of Lycoris: golden spider lily (*L. aurea*), white (*L. albiflora*), salmon/orange (*L. sanguinea*) and the light pink naked lily (*L. squamigera*).

Hurricane lilies are easy to grow. Just plant one bulb almost anywhere in your landscape and it will come up year after year, splitting itself into additional bulbs. Every couple of years dig up the bulbs and divide them. Plant in full sun to partial shade, average water, will reach 12-18 inches (30-45cm), bloom late summer early autumn for about 2 weeks. Excellent in cut flower arrangements. Propagate by dividing bulb clumps in early summer when the plant is dormant.

Danger: Parts of plant are poisonous if ingested

SPIDER LILIES

Family: *Amaryllidaceae*

Genus: *Hymenocallis*

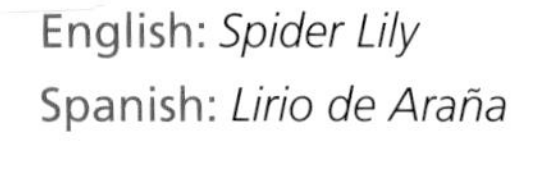

English: *Spider Lily*

Spanish: *Lirio de Araña*

The genus *Hymenocallis* is native to the New World, occurring from the lower Mississippi Valley and Southern United States through Central America and the Caribbean. The flowers are white, with a pronounced staminal cup and narrow tepal segments (petals and sepals). The members of the genus are often called Spider Lilies and it is unclear at this time how many species exist.

Plant in full sun to partial shade, will reach 24-48inches (60-120cm), high moisture needs, do not let dry out between waterings, suitable for water gardens, blooms spring to early autumn, propagate by dividing bulbs. Can use seed but slow flowering, also seed does not store well.

SPIDER LILY
Hymenocallis caribaea

GALVESTON SPIDER LILY
Hymenocallis galvestonenis

English: *Spider Plant, Spider Ivy, Ribbon Plant, Hen-and-Chickens*

Spanish: *Planta de Cinta, Mala Madre, Planta de Araña*

Zulu: *Iphamba. Umhlambezo*

SPIDER PLANT

Family: *Liliaceae*

Chlorophytum comosum

From South Africa, there are more than 200 species in the genus *Chlorophytum*; all are evergreen perennials, but only a couple are regularly cultivated. The spider plant is one of the most popular indoor plants of all time. The wild species has green leaves, but most cultivars are variegated with the roots and rhizomes serving as water storage organs during dry periods.

After blooming and fruiting, baby spider plants develop on the stalks. These little 'spiders' or plantlets take root wherever they touch the ground and can form clumps 3ft. (1m) tall and across, with stems cascading out as much as 5ft. (1.5m).

Plant in sun to light shade, needs afternoon shade, will reach 18-24inches (45-60cm), requires consistently moist soil, do not let dry out between waterings, white blooms spring through summer. Propagate by dividing the rootball or the plantlets that develop on the elongated stalks can be rooted easily. Bag seedheads to capture ripening seed, allow pods to dry on plant then break open to collect seeds.

Grown for its interesting foliage, groundcover, borders and edging, does well in containers, suitable for growing indoors, perfect for hanging baskets.

Danger: All parts of this plant are poisonous if ingested.

TIGER LILY

Family: *Liliaceae*

Lilium lancifolium

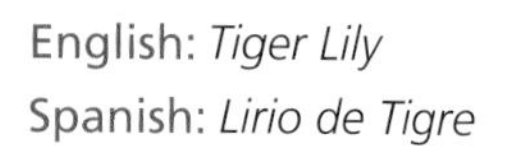

English: *Tiger Lily*
Spanish: *Lirio de Tigre*

From China and Japan this outrageous lily has been around for at least 2,000 years. Used as a food crop in China, where the scales from the bulbs were peeled, seasoned and cooked. Brought to Europe in the 15th century by the Dutch East India Company, then on to the Americas by the 1830's, and is now considered by many as an American wildflower.

Plant in full sun to partial shade, average water, will reach 4-6ft. (1.2-1.8m), blooms mid summer into autumn, scented flowers are down-facing, easy to grow and naturalize, late blooming, propagate by seed or by dividing bulbs (including offsets) —small bulbuls in the leaf axils on the upper part of the stems are quite easy to propagate, or by dividing the bulb's scales. Seed collecting, allow seedheads to dry on plants then remove and collect seeds.

A long-time garden favourite, tallest of the lilies with an abundance of blooms.

English: *Rain Lily, Fairy Lily, Zephyr Lily*
Spanish: *Lirio de Lluvia*

WHITE RAIN LILY

Family: *Liliaceae*

Zephyranthes candida

Introduced in 1515 from Argentina and now widely naturalized. One of the hardiest, rain lilies are in a group of bulbous perennials found in grasslands from North to South America. They are grown for their erect, funnel-shaped, and crocus-like flowers. Rain lilies flower from late spring to autumn or when the foliage emerges from the soil, usually a few days after a rainstorm. This white Zeph is very common and is an early spring bloomer in the southeast United States. Plant in full sun to partial shade, average water, will reach 12-18 inches (30-45cm), although 6-8inches (15-20cm) is more common, bloom late spring into mid autumn. Propagate by dividing bulbs or from seed, direct sow outdoors in autumn. Seed collecting, allow seedheads to dry on plants then remove and collect.

Chapter 7
Orchids

Family: *Orchidaceae*

Spanish: *Orquídea*

Orchids boast a profound beauty—originating some 120 million years ago, they have proliferated and spread throughout the world, with over 1000 described genera and some 25,000 to 30,000 varieties of orchids in the forests, that is, naturally occurring orchids, and perhaps another 60,000 hybrids and varieties produced by horticulturists. Their colours can be very subtle to quite astonishing, while their shapes visually seem to have a deep sensual, almost sexual appeal. Their name is derived from the Greek *'orchis'*, meaning *"testicle"*—from the appearance of structures called pseudobulbs. The vast majority of orchids are epiphytic or "air" plants that need no soil, have minute seeds, and bilaterally symmetrical flowers with three petals, one of which is lip-shaped.

There are many types of specialization's within the Orchidaceae. Best known are the seemingly endless structural variations in the flowers that encourage pollination by particular species of insects, bats, or birds.

Our obsession can be traced back to ancient civilizations, and has generated an entire "culture" surrounding the orchid, that includes gardening techniques, vast numbers of scientific classifications, societies

and clubs of orchid hobbyists, trade expositions, a specialized vocabulary, literature and art—especially photography.

Whether munching on a vanilla ice-cream cone or biting into a piece of vanilla cake, many people experience their first orchid without even knowing it. Yes, vanilla is an orchid!

For choosing varieties and growing orchids you will have to do some research—local nurseries, the library, friends and neighbors, orchid clubs and of course the internet, will overload you with more information than you'll ever need to begin your fascination with these ancient plants.

All these orchids were photographed by Gregory Basco in the rainforests of Costa Rica. For photo and tour information: www.deepgreenphotography.com or www.fotoverdetours.com

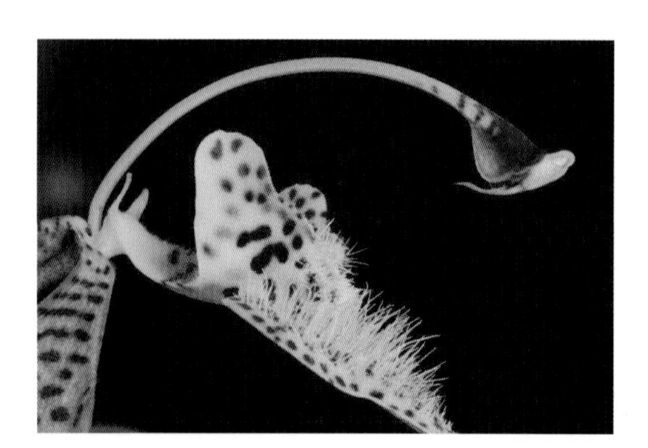

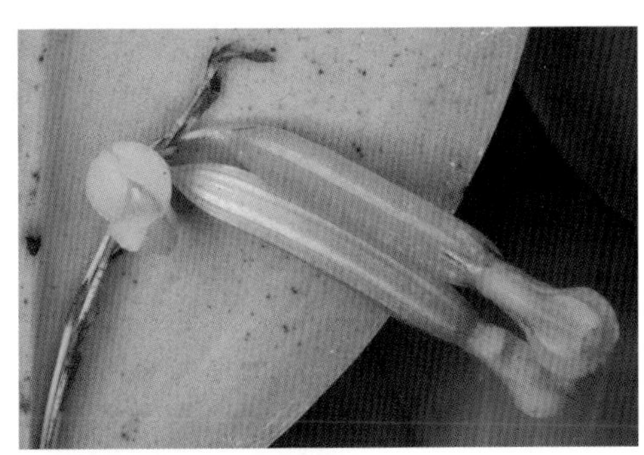

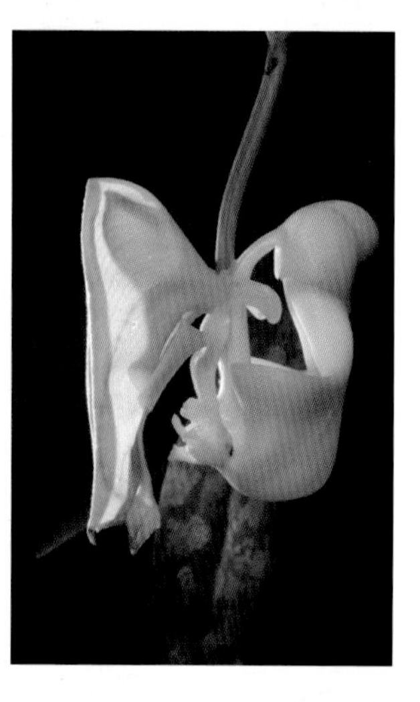

TROPICAL WATER GARDEN – SOUTH FLORIDA

Chapter 8
Ponds & Aquatics

Observed everywhere in ancient Egyptian art and life, made famous by Monet's water lily impressionist works in amazing hues of greens and blues, water lilies come to us through the ages and are most often the very reason for a water garden.

There are about 70 different species of water lilies, grouped into night, tropical and hardy varieties. Well adapted to their habitat they grow in and live on the edge of ponds, lakes and wetlands. All come in an astonishing array of colours.

Favouring tropical or hot climates, they receive their nutrition through photosynthesis so they need plenty of sunlight and space.

Night lilies bloom in the night, tropical lilies like the heat and bloom at all times of the day, while hardy lilies are able to withstand most conditions and are the most common.

The largest, the spectacular Giant Water Lily originates from the Amazon with leaves that can easily reach an astonishing 6ft. (1.8m) in diameter. Lilies have been used for food, medicine and even insect repellent. Many reproduce through the 'budding system' as mother plant roots detach in the mud and form new plants. They are vital producers of energy and food in water gardens and wetlands alike.

AQUATIC CANNA LILY

Family: *Cannaceae*

Canna glauca

English: *Canna Lily, Louisiana Canna*

Spanish: *Lirio de Aqua, Canna, Maraca Amarilla, Banderas*

Care-free and colourful, these South American natives, along with their hybrids and cultivars, are among the least fussy of water plants to grow and enjoy. The famed Longwood Cannas are the direct offspring of *Canna glauca*. In the early 1970's, Dr. Robert Armstrong crossed *Canna glauca* with terrestrial Canna hybrids. These offspring are identifiable because of their blue-green foliage, for which *Canna glauca* itself was named.

Plant in full sun to partial shade, on the margins of marshes, swamps, ponds, and wet ditches. Will reach 4-6ft. (1.2-1.8m), requires consistently moist soil, blooms almost constantly. Propagate by division of the root clump as the plant comes into growth in the spring.

English: *Golden Canna, Bandana of the Everglades*

Spanish: *Lirio de Oro, Canna, Banderas, Lirio de Pantano*

GOLDEN CANNA LILY

Family: *Cannaceae*

Canna flaccida

Bandana of the Everglades, is the only canna native to Florida, and lives in great profusion in the swamps and beside ponds. So much so it is sometimes considered to be an invasive. Still it's wonderfully fragrant, pale to bright lemon yellow blooms are a visual delight.

Plant in full sun to partial shade, will reach 36-48inches (90-120cm), blooms mid-summer through mid-autumn, requires consistently moist soil; do not let dry out between waterings, suitable for bogs and water gardens. Will grow in large pots or tubs. Attractive to bees and butterflies. Cold sensitive. Propagate by dividing rhizomes and tubers, best to dig up, dry and store rhizomes until the end of winter. From seed, sow indoors before last frost, germinate in a damp paper towel.

Seed collecting, allow pods to dry on plant, break open to collect seeds. The seed can live for over 600 years, in the ground, and will activate and sprout after a fire.

SACRED WATER LILY

Family: *Nelumbonaceae*

Nelumbo nucifera

English: *Egyptian Lotus, Sacred Waterlily, Sacred Lotus*

Spanish: *Lirio de Sagrado*

Australia, Indonesia and India are all given credit as the origin for this spectacular water plant, whose stunning, huge pink flowers will add dimension and grace to any pond garden.

Every part of the plant at some point in time and history has and is used from foods to traditional medicines, boiled, roasted, smoked, drunk as tea and used as a narcotic!

Quite easy to grow, plant in full sun to partial shade, seeds or roots must be firmly buried or sunk into a pond, creek or tub. Will survive winter if roots do not freeze. Will reach 4-6ft. (1.2-1.8m) reported in the wild as high as 20ft. (6m), blooms spring through summer, very high moisture needs! Propagate by dividing rhizomes or by seed. Seed collecting, allow pods to dry on plant then break open to collect seeds.

English: *Tropical Water Lily, Waterlily*
Spanish: *Lirio de Aqua*

TROPICAL WATER LILY

Family: *Nymphaeaceae*

Genus: *Nymphaea*

Made famous by Monet's canvases and French waterlily pioneer Joseph Marliac's hybridizing work, everyone can enjoy these amazing pond plants.

Tropical varieties are spectacular pond plants and like the temperature to be at least 70F (21C). The tropical waterlily dies off in the winter and does not come back at all in colder winter climates. Flowers are held high above water level, tend to be fuller, the colours more vibrant, and for the most part, very fragrant. Leaf edges of tropical pads tend to be serrated. Blooms open early morning and last through the day, there are also many Tropical Night-Blooming Water Lily hybrids available.

Hardy varieties of waterlilies are among the easiest pond plants to grow, flowers generally float on the surface of the water, die back in the winter then sprout new pads and flowers the following season. Leaf edges of the hardy pads are generally smooth.

If you live in areas that freeze, you can winter your tropical water lilies inside and bring them out again in the spring. Over-wintering water lilies requires a little, easily obtainable, information via the internet.

Plant in full sun to partial shade, check on depths and spreads when planning a water garden; blooms from mid-spring to mid-autumn. Very high moisture needs, propagate by division, leaf cuttings and from seed. Seed Collecting, bag seedheads to capture ripening seed, direct sow after last frost.

NIGHT BLOOMING WATER LILY

HARDY WATER LILY

CLASSIC ISLAND GARDEN – CAYMAN ISLANDS

Chapter 9
Shrubs

This chapter on shrubs could have doubled the size of the book without trying, so in keeping with the general philosophy of the book being a guide to the most likely species you would observe or grow in the geographical area—the choices were made and are shown.

The building blocks of any tropical garden, shrubs contain a huge and wide variety of plant species and cultivars. From exotics to dune stabilizers this chapter should not only help you identify the plants and flowers but give you ideas on sizes, colours, and choices for your own garden or greenhouse.

A Note On Jasmines:

There are about 200 species of Jasmines, all native to the Old World—India, Western China and other parts of Asia including Japan, Borneo, Thailand, and some South Seas islands—and members of the genus Jasminum are true Jasmines. The name 'jasmine' basically refers to many, and often unrelated, varieties of shrubs, vines and trees that have fragrant white flowers.

Jasmine perfumes are made from the flowers of several species, while Jasmine Tea is flavoured from Arabian Jasmine, which actually comes from South East Asia!.

Confederate (*Trachelospermum jasminoides*) and Chilean Jasmine (*Mandevilla laxa*) are in the Apocynaceae family; Night Blooming Jasmine (*Cestrum nocturnum*) is in the Solanaceae family; and South Carolina's state flower, Carolina Jasmine (*Gelsemium sempervirens*) is in the Loganiaceae family.

Jasmines can be found in the chapters on SHRUBS and VINES.

BIRD OF PARADISE

Family: *Strelitziaceae*

Strelitzia reginae

English: *Bird of Paradise, Crane Flower, Queens Bird of Paradise*

Spanish: *Estrelitzia, Paraíso de Ave*

Zulu: *Isagudu, Isigude*

A South African native, this exotic is a relative of the banana and it's outrageous flower is recognized worldwide. Inspiration for designers to architects and painters, it's hugely popular in flower arrangements.

There are several varieties of this plant, both in size of leaf, colour of leaf (some blue-green) and particularly in the flower. A few varieties have double flowers, some have flowers with an exceptional amount of red or vermilion at their base, and there is a rare yellow-leaf variety (collector's item).

Plant in full sun to partial shade, dislikes too much sun during the hottest part of the day. Height varies from 3-5ft. (1-1.5m), blooms late winter through early summer, but can flower throughout the year. Average water, propagate by seeds or clump division in spring. Seed collecting, allow pods to dry on the plant then break open to collect seeds.

Danger: Parts of this plant are poisonous if ingested.

MANDELA'S GOLD

English: *Blanket Flower, Indian Blanket, Rose Ring, Firewheel*

Spanish: *Flores de Cobija*

BLANKET FLOWER

Family: *Asteraceae*

Gaillardia pulchella

Named after the French botany patron M. Gaillard there are at least a dozen varieties of Gaillardia, most native to North America.

They bloom from mid spring through early autumn, will tolerate dry & salty conditions, and sandy soils, making them an attractive low maintenance choice for seaside plantings. Many states sow freeway and highway shoulders with blanket flowers, providing spectacular displays of colour. The showy flowers are perfect for cutting and most will last for about a week in water – a nature, home and garden favorite.

Plant in sun to partial shade, will reach 18-24inches (45-60cm), will reseed itself, is perfect for hanging baskets, easy grower, attractive to bees especially & butterflies, propagate from seed.

BLUE BUTTERFLY

Family: *Verbenaceae*

Clerodendrum ugandense

English: *Blue Butterfly Bush, Blue Glory Bower, Butterfly Clerodendrum*

Spanish: *Mariposa de Azul*

There are more than 400 species of Clerodendrum. The members of this diverse genus occur naturally in tropical and subtropical Asia and Africa, and include evergreen and deciduous trees, shrubs, vines and herbaceous plants. The genus name comes from the Greek: "*dendron*", tree; and "*kleros*", chance, a reference to the varied medicinal properties purported for some members of the genus.

This delightful shrub hails from Kenya and Uganda in East Africa, with the flowers resembling little butterflies in two different shades of blue.

Plant in sun to light shade, average water, will reach 8-10ft. (2.4-3m), blooms almost continuously from early spring through late autumn, propagate from stem or root cuttings, or from rooted suckers. Suitable for pots and indoors. This plant is attractive to bees, butterflies and birds. Prune as needed anytime. Bring indoors when temperatures approach freezing.

English: *Blue Ginger*
Spanish: *Gingibre de Azul*

BLUE GINGER

Family: *Commelinaceae*

Dichorisandra thyrsiflora

From Brazil, and not a true ginger, but a relative of the Purple Heart plant, it borrows the same characteristics of arching stems with deep green leaves as gingers. Topped on terminal spikes is a tight clustered vibrant violet blue flower with a white center and yellow eye

Plant in light shade, requires consistently moist soil, grown for foliage, will reach 6-8ft. (1.8-2.4m), blooms summer through autumn, propagate by dividing the root-ball and from herbaceous stem cuttings. Just cut pieces of the cane and stick in the ground. This plant is suitable for growing indoors. Grows wild all over Hawaii.

BRAZILIAN RED CLOAK

Family: *Acanthaceae*

Megaskepasma erythrochlamys

English: *Brazilian Red Cloak, Red Justicia, Brazilian Plume, Amazon Torch*

Spanish: *Capa de Rojo*

The genus encompasses about 300 species, mostly native to several regions of the subtropics, originating in Costa Rica, Nicaragua, El Salvador and Venezuela. A very showy shrub, the 'flower' consists of red bracts surrounding the true white flower. Two species are native to the Sonoran Desert and can take desert conditions. Most Justicias throughout the tropics and subtropics are pollinated by hummingbirds, some of which have beaks that exactly match the curve of the flower.

Plant in partial sun to shade, can take full sun but requires consistently moist soil, do not let it dry out between waterings, fast grower, will reach 12-15ft. (3.6-4.7m), winter bloomer, can bloom all year in a garden with proper fertilization, propagate from cuttings. This quick growing, large dense shrub is ideal for eliminating objectionable views!

English: *Bush Allamanda*
Spanish: *Allamanda de Arbusto*

BUSH ALLAMANDA

Family: *Apocynaceae*

Allamanda schottii

In the wonderful green and gold colour scheme of Brazil, where it originated, this shrub's golden flowers are it's signature. The genus name honours Frederich Allamand, an 18th. century Swiss botanist. There is also a vine Allamanda—see the chapter on Vines.

Plant in full sun to partial shade in most any decent soil. Requires consistently moist soil, do not let dry out between waterings, will reach 4-6ft. (1.2-1.8m), blooms repeatedly, propagate from cuttings or seed —allow pods to dry on plant then break open to collect seeds. Suitable for growing in containers and indoors. Likes hot and humid conditions—overwinter indoors in cold climates.

Danger: Handling the plant may cause skin irritation, the stems exude a toxic milky sap.

CANDLE BUSH

Family: *Fabaceae*

Senna alata

English: *Candle Bush, Empress Candle Plant, Candletree, Candelabra Bush*

Spanish: *Arbusto de Candelero*

More common names: Candlestick Senna, Wild Senna, Ringworm Cassia, Ringworm Tree, Emperor's Candlesticks.

Indigenous to Suriname where it is used in traditional medicine, this funky plant can be grown as a cultivated shrub 6-8ft. (1.8-2.4m) or small tree to 20-30ft. (6-9m).

Has exotic, erect, waxy, bright yellow spikes that resemble fat candles before the individual blossoms open. The fruit is a black pod with two broad wings, seeds are small, square and they rattle in the pod when ripe. A host plant to many species of sulphur caterpillars, and a favorite of bumblebees. Good butterfly garden shrub.

Plant in sun to partial shade, fast grower, blooms mid summer to mid autumn, drought-tolerant, self-sows freely or allow pods to dry on plant then break open to collect seeds. Propagate by dividing root-ball, cuttings or from seed.

Danger: Although used in alternative medicine, depending on species, many to all parts of the plant are poisonous if ingested.

Attracts fire ants—so be careful when cutting blooms and transplanting.

English: *Cockscomb, Plume Plant, Flamingo Celosia, Brain Flower*

Spanish: *Celosia*

CELOSIA

Family: *Amaranthaceae*

Celosia argentea var. cristata

Celosia argentea occurs widely as a weed in the equatorial tropics of Africa, Asia and South America. It may have originated in Asia and then spread to Africa and South America.

These popular annuals deliver long-lasting colour in the garden, from mid summer to mid autumn. Many varieties exist classified into several groups. These cultivars come with flowerheads in a variety of shapes and brilliant hot colours including red, orange, yellow, purple and creamy white. The flower-heads are actually hundreds of tiny flowers densely packed which usually stand above the foliage.

The Cristata Group cultivars were selected from mutations and are among the most bizarre of flowers. They make striking additions to fresh or dried arrangements, the dried flowerheads of all groups are excellent as they retain their colour and last indefinitely.

Celosias thrive in hot, humid weather, plant in full sun, easy to start from seed, average water, reach 24-36inches (60-90cm), make good container plants, attract bees, butterflies and birds. Seed collecting, collect seedhead/pod when flowers fade, allow to dry.

BOMBAY PURPLE
Celosia cristata

COCKSCOMB
Celosia argentea

CHENILLE PLANT

Family: *Euphorbiaceae*

Acalypha hispida

English: *Chenille Plant, Red-Hot Cat Tail, Monkey Tail, Pussy Tail*

Spanish: *Califa, Rabo de Gato, Roa de Mono*

Found throughout the West Indies and the South, this rather strange looking tropical shrub originates from the East Indies where it is used medicinally, although all parts of the plant are poisonous if ingested! It has dark green, veined pointed leaves and long velvety tails of dark red. The tails are made up of staminate flowers without petals and can grow to18inches (45cm) in length. The mature plant has leaves similar to Poinsettia, they're related (both are in the family: Euphorbiaceae).

Plant in bright but not direct sun, easy to grow, will reach 7-10ft. (2-3m), propagate via cuttings, root in half sand half peat, blooms repeatedly, prune to maintain, suitable for growing in pots and indoors.

Danger: All parts of the plant are poisonous if ingested.

CHEROKEE ROSE

Family: *Rosaceae*

Rosa laevigata

English: *Cherokee Rose, Snow-White Rose*
Spanish: *Rosa de Nivea*
State flower of Georgia.

Native to China this beautiful climbing rose has naturalized across much of the southeastern United States, and been selected as the state flower of Georgia.

It produces long, thorny, vinelike canes that will form a mound from 10-12ft. (3-4m) high and up to 15ft. (4.5m) wide. It will sprawl across other shrubs and trees for support, climbing to 30ft. (9m); and can be seen alongside roads, ditches and waterways.

The rose blooms briefly in early spring, with rows of fragrant white flowers densely arranged along the canes to form garlands of blossoms. The fruit is called a 'hip' (rose hips) which birds feast on for a vitamin C boost.

Plant in direct sun to partial shade, normal water, low maintenance, fast grower, drought and flood tolerant, propagate by dividing the rootball or by cuttings.

CORAL HIBISCUS

Family: *Malvaceae*

Hibiscus schizopetalus

This wonderful, frilled Hibiscus with the slender and gracefully curving stem is the parent of many hybrids. The petals are small, fringed and lacy, with the flower usually hanging downward. And it's those exquisitely delicate flowers that take your breath away. A tropical delight.

Plant in full sun to partial shade, average water, will reach 24-36inches (60-90 cm) but much higher if unpruned, to 8ft. (2.5m), blooms from late summer through autumn, propagate from cuttings.

Indoors, makes a great plant, requires ordinary potting soil, water generously once a week, and feed only a couple of times a year. It is a winter's delight!

English: *Fringed Hibiscus, Fuchsia Hibiscus, Coral Hibiscus, Chinese Lantern, Japanese Lanterns, Fringed Rosemallow, Waltzing Ladies*

Spanish: *Farolito de Chino, Arana, Canastilla, Paraguita China, Waitutu*

English: *Coral Plant, Physic Nut, Guatemala Rhubarb*

Spanish: *Planta de Coralino*

CORAL PLANT

Family: *Euphorbiaceae*

Jatropha multifida

Coral plant occurs naturally in Mexico, and southward through Central America to Brazil, and is part of the massive Euphorbiaceae family of some 8,000 species. Many of the euphorbs are succulents, and quite a few of them resemble cacti. Most have a poisonous milky latex sap—however their flowers are simply outrageous.

Plant in sun to partial shade, average water, self sows freely, propagate from cuttings in spring or sow seed outdoors in autumn, reaches an average height 6-8ft. (1.8-2.4m). Fairly fast growing, mid summer bloomer, makes a great container plant, suitable for growing indoors.

Danger: All parts of coral plant are very poisonous if ingested and the cloudy sap may irritate sensitive skin.

FIREBUSH

Family: *Rubiacea*e

Hamelia patens

English: *Firecracker Shrub, Mexican Firebush, Scarlet Bush, Hummingbird Bush*

Spanish: *Arbusto de Fuego, Cohete*

This showy vigorous growing shrub is native from central Florida south through the West Indies, Central America and down to Bolivia and Paraguay.

From indigenous islanders to modern researchers Firebush has a very wide range of medicinal uses. It's antifungul and antibacterial properties are well known for everything from skin diseases, rashes and insect stings to menstrual cramps, headaches and fevers. An amazing shrub.

Foliage colour is affected by the amount of sun the plant receives. Leaves are bright green if in a mostly shaded area, green tinged with scarlet if in partial sun, or deep scarlet if the plant is in full sun.

Plant in full sun to partial shade, make sure soil drains well, and requires extra water in the heat of summer, will reach 15ft. (4.6m), blooms profusely from late spring through early winter, attractive to butterflies, especially Zebra Longwings, and hummingbirds. The berries are relished by birds and other animals. Makes a great potted plant.

FIRECRACKER PLANT

Family: *Scrophulariaceae*

Russelia equisetiformis

English: *Firecracker Plant, Coral Plant, Coralblow, Fountain Plant*

Spanish: *Planta de Cohete*

Native to Mexico this wonderful multi-branched subshrub produces gorgeous hanging clusters of scarlet tubular flowers about an inch (2.5cm) long that look like little firecrackers, will spill over a fence or raised bed, does well on the patio and indoors in front of a window. A hanging basket of coral plant makes a great gift.

Plant in full sun to partial shade, average water, fast grower, will reach unchecked heights of 4-6ft. (1.2-1.8m), self sows freely, or propagate from stem cuttings, blooms almost continuously, attractive to bees, butterflies and hummingbirds.

FIRESPIKE

Family: *Acanthaceae*

Odontonema strictum

English: *Firespike, Cardinal Guard, Scarlet Flame*

Spanish: *Flamear de Escarlata*

This plant, native to Mexico and Central America, is grown for its beautiful deep green bushy tropical foliage and its magnificent glow-in-the dark red blooms. Gardeners consistently praise it for wonderful colour in the shade and easy propagation. A winning winter bloomer.

Plant in full sun to partial shade and moist well drained soil, average water, will reach 6-8ft. (1.8-2.5m), once established it can tolerate all but the longest droughts, propagate from cuttings or seed, attractive to bees, hummingbirds and all kinds of butterflies. A must for butterfly and hummingbird gardens.

English: *Starburst Bush, Shooting Star, Fireworks*

Spanish: *Pirotecnia*

FIREWORKS

Family: *Verbenaceae*

Clerodendrum quadriloculare

The genus Clerodendrum consists of over 450 species of trees or shrubs. The name is derived from the Greek 'kleros' or chance, and 'dendron' a tree; and is supposed to be in reference to the variable medicinal qualities of plants in this genus.

Originally from the Philippines, Fireworks is an apt name as the blossoms burst forth in sprays of pink tubes ending with a smaller spray of creamy white flowers. Blooms are huge, with each flower made up of scores of smaller ones. A 'show stopper' in any garden.

This plant will grow as either a large shrub or small tree. Plant in full sun to partial shade, keep moist, will reach 12-15ft. (3.5-4.5m), blooms late winter through early summer, attractive to bees and butterflies May be considered an invasive in some areas.

GARDENIA

Family: *Rubiaceae*

Gardenia jasminoides or angusta

English: *Gardenia, Cape Jasmine*

Spanish: *Gardenia*

Gardenia is a lovely shrub from South China whose fragrance is legendary, the powerful sweet fragrance can fill an entire home. Gardenias are evergreens and the pure white flowers are gorgeous, rose-like at their peak of appearance. Starting out white and fading to cream then brown, blooms appear from late spring through mid summer and make excellent cut flowers. They have been traditional corsage flowers for many years. Float cut flowers in shallow designer bowls indoors—tres chic.

Plant in full sun to partial shade, prefer acid, moist, well-drained soils, like humidity and moisture, will reach 8ft. (2.5m), read up on fertilizing, propagate from softwood cuttings or simple layering. Suffer from several pest problems. Cold sensitive —winter indoors in cold climates. Will grow in pots and indoors. Amazing fragrance. Traditional symbol of the American deep south. A winner.

English: *Giant Star Potato Tree, Giant Potato Tree, Prairie Potato*

Spanish: *Papa Tropical, Papa Gigante*

GIANT STAR POTATO TREE

Family: *Solanacea*

Solanum macranthum

The Solanum family is very large, consisting of nearly 1500 species ranging from vegetables like the potato and eggplants, to ornamental shrubs and climbers, plus a number of weeds.

From tropical South America this is an attractive fast growing bushy shrub or small tree. Not a true potato, Giant Potato Trees are widely cultivated in the tropics for ornamental purposes. The leaves are evergreen, large, lobed and prickly, while flowers are fragrant and change their colour from white to lavender to purple.

Plant in full sun, fast grower, will reach 15ft. (4.7m), requires consistently rich, moist soil, do not let dry out between waterings, blooms repeatedly all year round, tri-colour blooms, propagate from seed. Suitable for planting singly, keep above 35F (1.7C).

Danger: Parts of plant are poisonous if ingested.

GLORY BUSH or PRINCESS FLOWER

Family: *Melastomataceae*

Tibouchina urvilleana

English: *Glory Bush, Princess Flower*
Spanish: *Arbusto de Gloria, Flora de Princesa*

Native to Brazil, Tibouchina is a very popular landscape plant in frost free areas around the world. Covered with wonderful purple flowers most of the year, with a big summer show!

Tibouchina granulosa is a tropical tree native to Brazil and Bolivia and reaches 40ft. (12m). *Tibouchina heteromalla* is a small shrub about 3ft. (90cm), and there are also numerous hybrids.

Plant in full sun, average water, fast grower, will reach 12-15ft. (3.6-4.7m), propagate from softwood cuttings, fertilize after each blooming period, and with some good pruning, Tibouchina can be the best plant on your block!

English: *Hibiscus*

Spanish: *Hibisco, Mar Pacifico, Pabonas, Hibisco Hawaiano*

State flower of Hawaii.

HIBISCUS

Family: *Malvaceae*

Hibiscus rosa-sinensis

One of the classic and beautiful signature flowers of the tropics, Hibiscus is perhaps the best known tropical shrub and flower in the world. The five petal, five stigma, five lobe to calyx form of the flower is known everywhere with hundreds of hybrids, and even mini-hybrids, to enjoy in every colour imaginable.

Ancient and of vague origin, nobody knows whether the Hibiscus really is a native of China as its Latin name, *rosa-sinensis* (Chinese Rose), suggests. India is also an origin candidate. Cultivated in Europe for centuries, some feel that the modern Hibiscus *rosa-sinensis* is not a natural species at all but a collection of man-made hybrids.

The flower from any Hibiscus, whether on or off the plant, will remain fresh all day, and then wilt in the evening. If needed for decoration at night buds should be cut early and kept refrigerated. Buds picked the

HAWAIIAN SUNSET
Cultivar

night before will open fully the next morning. Flowers are produced all year round, but the best production is during the autumn and spring when temperatures are moderate. A cutting when placed in water for a few weeks, will readily root.

Often called the Queen of Shrubs, throughout the world the Hibiscus furnishes beauty, food, medicine, perfume and dye—a lovely gift from nature.

Plant in full sun, likes water, let dry out between waterings, will reach 15ft. (4.5m), blooms repeatedly, propagate from softwood cuttings. Seed collecting, bag seedheads to capture ripening seed. Make great container and indoor plants, robust, easy care, attract birds and butterflies.

HARDY HIBISCUS
Hibiscus moscheutos

SYLVIA GOODMAN
Cultivar

FRAGILE HIBISCUS

▲ ROSE OF SHARON ▶
Hibiscus syriacus

WILD HIBISCUS
Hibiscus pedunculatus

INKBERRY

Family: *Goodeniaceae*

Scaevola plumieri

English: *Inkberry, Half Flower, Fan Flower, Waxy Bush, Beachberry, Gullfeed*

Spanish: *Naupaka, Lechuga, Baya Tinta, Baya Grano, Baya de la Playa*

Originating in the Australia / Oceania areas, over eons, drift seeds made it to Africa, the Pacific Islands, Caribbean, and Gulf of Mexico. A native of the holly family and found on tropical beaches, dunes, barrier islands and coastal habitats, Inkberry is considered a native plant in the SE United States.

Very popular, Inkberries can endure salt, drought, wind and sun acting as a strand stabilizing plant with root suckers forming new colonies. It's great for oceanfront landscaping with the black olive sized berries as food for wildlife, while the roots have been used in home medicinal remedies.

Plant in full sun to partial shade, average water, slow grower, will reach to 4-6ft. (1.2-1.8m), blooms late spring through early autumn, fanlike half flowers, salt tolerant, drought tolerant, suitable for xeriscaping, will stabilize sand dunes, propagate from seed and stems that have rooted naturally. Requires both male and female plants to fruit. Bees are the primary pollinators.

Note: Listed as threatened by the state of Florida, this plant may be considered a protected species in other areas too. Check before digging or collecting.

English: *Jungle Geranium, Flame of the Woods, Jungle Flame*

Spanish: *Santa Rita, Ixora Guillermina, Cruz de Malta*

IXORA

Family: *Rubiaceae*

Ixora

Related to the gardenia and a member of the coffee family from the East Indies, and whose name derives from an Indian deity, there are about 400 species of this fabulous shrub. Very popular in the tropics were it blooms all year long in pink, red, orange, yellow or purple colours and is used as "the" hedge shrub. Maximum beauty is from late spring through early winter.

Plant in full sun, will reach 36-48inches (90-120cm), average water, will tolerate salt spray, propagate from stem cuttings. Best to use Ixora coccinea for hedges. Cut flower stems are long lasting and effective in arrangements.

IXORA HEDGE
Ixora coccinea

IXORA HEDGE FLOWER

IXORA NORA GRANT

SUPER KING
Ixora casei

ORANGE IXORA

LAKEVIEW JASMINE

Family: *Rutaceae*

Murraya paniculata

English: *Lakeview Jasmine, Orange Jessamine, Chinese Box*

Spanish: *Jazmin*

Originally found from India to Malaysia and southeast Asia this is a must for fragrant flower lovers. Orange Jessamine is often sold as 'Jasmine' but is not a true jasmine. It will produce bunches of white fragrant flowers making it very attractive to bees, butterflies and birds.

Plant in light shade, requires consistently moist soil, will reach 10-12ft. (3-3.6m) outdoors, blooms repeatedly from spring through autumn, propagate from semi-hardwood cuttings and seed. This plant is suitable for growing indoors, makes great container plant, used in bonsai. The fragrance is intoxicating.

English: *Lantana, Ham & Eggs, Shrub Verbena*
Spanish: *Lantana, Huevo con Jamon, Verbena*

LANTANA

Family: *Verbenaceae*

Lantana camara

Between several species and multiple hybrids there are at least 20 varieties of this hardy plant. Native to the Caribbean, Lantanais drought-resistant, deer-resistant, bug-proof, vigorous and blooms from spring to autumn. It can handle salt and beach conditions and in some areas is considered an invasive weed. However gardeners love it and the bright coloured blooms standout adding blocks of colour.

Plant in full sun to partial shade, average water, will reach an average of 36-48inches (90-120cm), propagate from cuttings or seed, is attractive to bees and especially butterflies. Good in containers and green-houses—a must in butterfly gardens.

Aroma—some people find the blossoms aromatic and spicy, while the Malay and Chinese name for Lantana means "chicken droppings flower"!!

Danger: All parts of this plant are poisonous if eaten and can be fatal. Handling the plant may cause skin irritation, wear gloves and wash your hands afterwards. Do not grow indoors.

LANTANA
Lantana camara

English: *Annatto, Lipstick Plant, Urucum, Lipstick Tree*

Spanish: *Achote, Annato, Achiote, Bija, Chaya*

LIPSTICK PLANT

Family: *Bixaceae*

Bixa orellana

Native to the West Indies and South America, Annato is a multi-valued plant. As an ornamental, food and fabric dye, condiment, in cosmetics, body paint, and in traditional medicine, this plant stands alone in its family, plus can reach an age of 50 years.

Although it doesn't produce an edible fruit, the red spiny pods are a fruit, the Annatto is widely grown for the small reddish-orange seeds inside the radical, prickly, heartshaped pods; the seeds are crushed, the dye used to colour butter and cheese, and in Latin America to colour rice and other foods.

Plant in full sun to partial shade, regular water, can reach 20ft. (6m), propagate easily by cuttings or seed: seeds take longer to bloom. When fully mature, the fruit split open exposing the numerous seeds. Blooms are 3inches (7cm) in pink or white.

MUSSAENDA

Family: *Rubiaceae*

Mussaenda erythrophylla

English: *Mussaenda, Ashanti Blood, Red Flag Bush, Tropical Dogwood*

Spanish: *Mussaenda*

An evergreen shrub related to coffee trees, Mussaenda has many parts of the world from tropical Asia, tropical Africa and the West Indies claiming origin. The white one is originally from the Philippines and is known as 'Dona Aurora' and the peach/pink one 'Dona Luz'. Both cultivars were named after former Philippine First Ladies.

The plant's colour comes from bracts and not the small flowers at the center of each bract. Colours include rose, white, red, pale pink and some mixtures. This is the same colour-producing system used by tropicals like Heliconia and Bougainvillea.

Plant in sun to partial shade, the white prefers partial shade, reaches10ft. (3m) although 30ft. (9m) has been reported in the wild, average water, likes humidity, propagate from cuttings. Blooms repeatedly from late winter to mid autumn depending on zone. Prune heavily in late autumn to late winter. This will contribute to shape and produce many more branch tips and flowering bracts.

WHITE: DONA AURORA
Mussaenda philippica

English: *Virgin Tree, Tropical Dogwood*

Spanish: *Mussaenda*

English: *Natal Plum, Boxwood*
Spanish: *Bujeta, Macrocarpa*
Zulu: *Umthungulu*

NATAL PLUM

Family: *Apocynaceae*

Carissa macrocarpa

Native to KwaZulu-Natal, South Africa, this shrub is one of the most popular hedge shrubs in the world. Easily groomed into about any shape you want, Natal Plum has dense foliage for screening, sharp thorns to discourage, flowers with a wonderful jasmine-like scent, and edible fruit!

There are many variations including dwarf and thornless varieties. Macrocarpa will grow to 6-8ft. (1.8-2.4m) and bloom throughout the year. Make good container plants. Very good for oceanside cover, security and ground support.

Plant in full sun to partial shade, average water, drought tolerant, salt spray resistant, propagate by cuttings, seed collecting is not recommended for this plant.

Danger: Although the ripe fruit is edible all other parts of the plant are poisonous if ingested. Plant has very sharp spines so use extreme caution when handling.

OLEANDER

Family: *Apocynaceae*

Nerium oleander

English: *Oleander, Rose Bay*

Spanish: *Adelfa, Rosa Francesa*

A member of the Periwinkle family native to northern Africa, the eastern Mediterranean basin and Asia Minor, this shrub is a fast growing, hardy, versatile, evergreen popular with tropical gardeners for it's abundant showy flowers in white, red, pink, salmon and even pale yellow that come in single, double or five petal formations. There are several varieties and cultivars including dwarfs, many are delightfully fragrant.

Plant in full sun to partial shade, likes warm humid conditions but can survive both drought and flood conditions, easy fast grower, will reach 20ft. (6m) unchecked, prune for shape and bloom quantity, blooms spring through autumn, propagate from cuttings or this species commonly produces many side shoots which can be replanted in their own pots. Also by seed, but selected cultivars may not grow true to form. Can be grown in pots and indoors but is poisonous.

*Danger: this shrub is toxic—***poisonous***—and even food cooked on the wood can be poisonous. Contact with skin may cause a reaction. Avoid smoke when burning cuttings. Do not use in playgrounds or children play areas. Wear gloves when handling.*

Also lookout for the Oleander caterpillar —do not touch. Can be identified by pale orange colour, white spots, with both long and short hairs.

WHITE OLEANDER

PINK OLEANDER

RED OLEANDER

PAGODA FLOWER

Family: *Verbenaceae*

Clerodendron speciosissimum

English: *Pagoda Flower, Clerodendron, Glorybower, Flaming Glorybower, Java Glorybower*

Spanish: *Guardia Civil, Cógetelo Todo*

A native to Java, these shrubs have large heart shaped, thick, velvety leaves and large flower 'pagodas' which flower throughout the year in frost free climates. The fabulous flower pagodas are made up of small individual flowers, stamens and pistils that curve beyond the flower, and small, shiny, berrylike fruit. Popular throughout the Caribbean and Florida, there are at least eight species of pagoda flower.

Pagodas are attractive to bees, butterflies and birds, a boon for gardens, nature lovers and photographers alike. They are cultivated for the ornamental value of their 'pagoda' flowers and it's shape is even used as inspiration for jewelry designs.

Plant in full sun to partial shade, will reach up to 6ft. (1.8m), and have been found in Java to 12ft. (3.6m). A fast grower, this plant loves warm and humid conditions. In cooler zones it will die back and re-emerge in the spring. Propagate with seeds or cuttings, makes an excellent container and house plant.

PENTAS

Family: *Rubiaceae*

Pentas lanceolata

English: *Egyptian Star Cluster, Star Flower, Pentas*

Spanish: *Pentas*

Africa seems to be the original home of pentas, whose dark green leaves and prolific clusters of never-ending, five-petal flowers make it a garden favorite. Blooms may be red, white, lavender, purple, pink or even two-toned. All are extremely attractive to butterflies, bees and especially hummingbirds. Great for butterfly gardens.

Plant in full sun to partial shade, average water, will reach 36inches (90cm), blooms all year, propagate from stem cuttings. This plant is suitable for growing indoors, makes an ideal container plant.

PINK PENTAS

English: *Pinwheel Jasmine, Crape Jasmine, Crepe Jasmine*

Spanish: *Jazmin*

PINWHEEL JASMINE

Family: *Apocynaceae*

Tabernaemontana divaricata

Crape or Pinwheel Jasmine is native to tropical areas of India and is widely grown for its ornamental value in frost-free areas around the world. A frequently encountered cultivar is "*Flore Pleno*" which has double flowers. The waxy blossoms are white, five-petal pinwheels that are borne in small clusters on the stem tips.

This beautiful tropical shrub's rather fast rate of growth makes it a good plant for new gardens. It's feature is a delightful fragrance, even the foliage is aromatic and the leaves have been used to make black eye shadow! Best enjoyed in the evening —the scent is vaporized from the flowers by the heat of day.

Plant in sun to partial shade, average water, will reach 4-6ft. (1.2-1.8m), blooms from spring into summer, blooms repeatedly, propagate from softwood cuttings, prune lightly as required to maintain nice form.

PLUMBAGO

Family: *Plumbaginaceae*

Plumbago capensis *or Plumbago auriculata*

English: *Plumbago, Leadwort, Skyflower, Cape Leadwort*

Spanish: *Plombagina*

Zulu: *Umasheleshele; Umasweliswelі, Umatshintshine*

Cape Plumbago is a native of South Africa, an irregular evergreen shrub that will grow as a vine if pruned and trained or tied to a trellis. Plumbago bears spikes of flowers almost all year long in all shades of blue as well as a lovely, pure white cultivar. Responds well to heavy pruning to keep neat and maximize flowering.

Plant in direct sun to partial shade, very easy to grow, normal water, will reach 4ft. (1.25m), takes little or no maintenance. Once established is drought tolerant and is deer resistant. Propagate by dividing the rootball suckers, by root cuttings or semi-hardwood cuttings in spring. Grows well in containers, a favorite of butterflies, fast growing, low maintenance, always smiling.

Special notes: The tube of each flower is covered with sticky hairs, making it easy for the flowers to rest in one's hair or clothes for a little island color. Buy plants in bloom to get the shade of blue you desire.

Danger: All parts of the plant are poisonous if ingested.

English: *Poinsettia, Christmas Eve Flower*
Spanish: *Flor de Nochebuena, Flor de Pascuas*

POINSETTIA

Family: *Euphorbiaceae*

Euphorbia pulcherrima

The flower that is the symbol of Christmas has a fascinating history. Native to south-central Mexico the plant was favoured by Aztec kings and warriors alike. A symbol of new life for Aztec warriors killed in battle, they believed they would return to earth as butterflies or hummingbirds and drink from the poinsettia plant.

After Spanish colonization, Franciscan priests used poinsettia plants to decorate their nativity scenes—and thus poinsettias began their association with Christmas.

The plant was first introduced to the United States by US ambassador to Mexico, Joel Poinsett, who in 1825 brought them home to South Carolina where he began cultivating them, ultimately his name became the flower's name.

WHITE POINSETTIA
Cultivar

Poinsettias are not disposable plants but grow well in tropical garden and indoor alike. The red and pink colours of the plant are not the flower but a coloured bract, tiny yellow or green flowers can be found at the centre of each bract.

Cultivators in recent years have created more showier plants with colours now ranging from white to burgundy, bi-coloured and even 'splashed' with contrasting colours.

Plant in full sun to partial shade, average water, can reach an unchecked height of 12ft. (3.6m) or more. Bloom almost continuously if cut back once or twice a year. Propagate from stem cuttings, bag seedheads to capture ripening seed.

Danger: Parts of plant are poisonous if ingested.

PURPLE HEART

Family: *Commelinaceae*

Tradescantia pallida

English: *Purple Heart, Purple Queen, Wandering Jew*

Spanish: *Zebrina*

One of the most common fast growing ground covers, Zebrinas are also a relatively popular house plant. It is not as robust as one would think, breaking easily, but it does little harm and just comes back stronger. The flowers are tiny inconspicuous white to pink to lavender purple three petal jobs.

Plant almost anywhere, works in the ground, water and hanging baskets. Drought-tolerant, suitable for xeriscaping and growing indoors. Will reach 12-18inches (30-45cm), blooms all year, propagate from cuttings and layerings. Seed collecting is not recommended for this plant. Easy to grow, lasts forever.

Danger: Handling plant may cause skin irritation or allergic reaction.

Purple Heart Cultivar

RUELLIA or MEXICAN PETUNIA

Family: *Acanthaceae*

Ruellia brittoniana

English: *Desert Petunia, Florida Bluebells, Mexican Petunia, Mexican Blue Bells*

Spanish: *Ruellia*

Natives of tropical South America there are at least a dozen varieties including a dwarf variation. Known for their beautiful flowers and attractive foliage, Mexican Petunias are one of the easiest plants to grow. Prolific bloomers, in pink, purple and white.

Plant in sun to partial shade, will reach 24-48 inches (60-120cm) depending on species. Blooms repeatedly from summer through early autumn, drought tolerant and hummingbird friendly, propagate by dividing the rootball, stem cuttings or seed in spring—however they self seed profusely, considered an invasive in Florida.

English: *Shrimp Plant, Shrimp Bush*
Spanish: *Cola de Camarón*

SHRIMP PLANT

Family: *Acanthaceae*

Justicia brandegeana

A native from Mexico this shrub is an easy fast growing exotic. The array of arched, overlapping heart shaped bracts resembles a shrimp tail—hence Shrimp Plant! The bracts, up to 6inches (15cm) long, in salmon, rose-pink as well as pale yellow surround the tiny white flowers. A blooming summer favorite.

Plant in light shade, requires consistently moist soil, will easily reach 3-4ft. (90-120cm), prune regularly to produce flowers all year round in warm climates, propagate from cuttings, layerings or divide clumps. Use to create a mass of colour.

SHRIMP PLANT
Yellow

THRYALLIS

Family: *Malpighiaceae*

Galphimia glauca

English: *Golden Thryallis, Shower of Gold, Rain of Gold, Yellow Plumbago*

Spanish: *Lluvia de Oro*

Native to the tropical regions of Mexico to Guatemala where it blooms almost all year round, Thryallis is a tropical garden favorite.

It forms dense barriers that are attractive and functional, is a good candidate for low-maintenance landscapes, easy to grow, drought resistant, and useful for preventing hillside erosion. This shrub is one of the best for shearing into low hedges, does well in pots, greenhouses and conservatories.

Plant in sun to partial shade, average water, reaches 4-6ft. (1.2-1.8m), pruning in early spring produces bright yellow blooms from mid summer to mid autumn, propagate from cuttings. A fast grower and great summer flowerier.

TROPICAL MILKWEED

Family: *Asclepiadaceae*

Asclepias curassavica

English: *Tropical Milkweed, Bloodflower, Swallow-wort, Butterfly Weed, Mexican Milkweed, Scarlet Milkweed*

Spanish: *Hierba Leche*

Butterflies from all over your neighborhood will flock to the brilliantly coloured flowers of this South America native which has become a naturalized weed in tropical and subtropical pastures, fields and disturbed areas throughout the world, including central and southern Florida.

Milkweed is essential for the existence of Monarch butterflies. Butterflies and other nectar-sipping insects are attracted to the blossoms, and both Monarch and Queen butterflies lay their eggs on scarlet milk-weed.

The fruits are spindle shaped pods, 3-4inches (7.6-10.2cm) long, that eventually split open to release little flat seeds that drift away on silky parachutes. The dried pods are used in arrangements.

Very easy to grow, plant in full sun to partial shade, will reach 36-48inches (90-120cm), average water, blooms continuously from spring through early autumn, propagate by division or can be started from cuttings, grows quickly from seed.

Seed collecting, bag seedheads to capture ripening seed, allow pods to dry on plant then break open to collect seeds. Properly cleaned, seed can be successfully stored.

Danger: All milkweeds are poisonous if ingested, and the milky sap is a skin irritant. The butterflies whose caterpillars feed on milkweeds contain the same poisonous glycosides and are poisonous as well.

TURK'S CAP

Family: *Malvaceae*

Malvaviscus arboreus

English: *Sleeping Hibiscus, Pepper Hibiscus, Wax Mallow, Ladies Teardrop, Wild Fuchsia, Scotchman's Purse and Turk's Fez or Cap!*

Spanish: *Hibisco de Durmiente*

A robust shrub that blooms on and off throughout the year with it's best show of flamboyant red flowers coming at the Christmas holiday season. The entire plant resembles the hibiscus, a close relative, with the flowers resembling a red Shriner's or Turk's Fez.

Can grow to10ft. (3m) in height, take direct sun or if grown in shade often becomes vine like with stems that climb up adjacent trees and bushes. Needs to be severely pruned in spring because, like hibiscus, it blooms on new growth only. Is attractive to bees, butterflies and birds. Average water, propagate by dividing the rootball or from semi-hardwood cuttings, or allow seed-heads to dry on plants then remove and collect seeds

Plant seed indoors before last frost and outdoors direct sow after last frost. Fun.

YELLOW ELDER

Family: *Bignoniaceae*

Tecoma stans var. angustata

English: *Yellow Elder, Trumpetbush, Ginger-Thomas, Gold Star Esperanza*

Spanish: *Saúco Amarillo, Roble Amarillo, Ruibarba, San Andrés, Copete, Fresnillo*

Native to both tropical and sub-tropical America, Yellow Elder appears in a number of variations. The tree variety grows to 25ft. (7.6m), the shrub 10-12ft. (3-3.6m), with further varieties just 3-4ft. (1-1.2m), and there are also varieties with orange flowers.

However it's the clusters of cheerful yellow flowers that bloom year round along with it's delicate champagne fragrance that make this plant a tropical winner. It has been used in a variety of purposes in herbal medicine from diabetes to the common cold and has catnip like ingredients that feline's fancy.

Plant in full sun, average water, attractive to bees and butterflies, propagate from seed or stem cuttings, deer resistant. Makes a great potted patio shrub Yellow Elder is a best possible selection for any garden, its perfect for any tropical and subtropical yard. Easy to grow, a winner.

Official Flower – United States Virgin Islands & Bahamas

YELLOW JACOBINIA

Family: *Acanthaceae*

Justicia aurea

English: *Yellow Jacobinia, Brazilian Plume, King's Crown, Plume Flower*

Spanish: *Jacobinia, Justicia*

Justicias have been popular container and greenhouse plants since the early nineteenth century when they were raised in Victorian conservatories.

Native to South America, these shade lovers are a perfect choice for bringing dazzling colour to the darker areas of your garden. In summer the plant covers itself with large showy spikes of flowers in shades from white, pink, red, orange, purple and yellow.

Plant in light to full shade, average water, will reach 4-6ft. (1.2-1.8m), blooms summer through early autumn, easy to propagate from softwood cuttings. Make good pot, container and indoor plants, winter indoors. Inexpensive and easy to grow—a winner.

YESTERDAY, TODAY AND TOMORROW

Family: *Solanaceae*

Brunfelsia pauciflora

English: *Yesterday, Today and Tomorrow*
Spanish: *Ayer, Hoy y Manana*

This native from Brazil is named for it's three different colours of wonderfully fragrant flowers. First blooms are deep lilac which turn to light lavender and finish with a fade to white. Hence the names yesterday = deep lilac, today = lavender and tomorrow = white.

Plant in full sun to partial shade, average water, reaches 4-6ft. (1.2-1.8m), blooms repeatedly, prune back heavily twice a year to maximize tips and bloom quantity. Propagate by cuttings or allow seedheads to dry on plants then remove and collect seeds.

Great in hanging baskets, pots, indoors and greenhouses—a lovely plant.

Danger: Seed is poisonous if ingested.

BOUGAINVILLEA – ANSE CHASTANET – ST. LUCIA

Chapter 10
Vines

There is something quite wonderful and a little creepy about vines, perhaps as they are often termed *creepers* and from the past—those old black and white horror movies—to the present Harry Potter adventures, heroes and villains alike are forever being snared, entangled and strangled in them! Ironically some like the Dutchman's Pipe with it's 'unique' aroma for attracting flies is quite creepy.

Fortunately however the vast majority of tropical vines are a sheer delight with volumes of cascading colour that boldly brighten any garden fence, wall, trellis, tree or frame, with Bougainvillea being the signature vine in tropical climates.

A note on Jasmines:

There are about 200 species of Jasmines, all native to the Old World—India, Western China and other parts of Asia including Japan, Borneo, Thailand, and some South Seas islands—and members of the genus Jasminum are true Jasmines. The name 'jasmine' basically refers to many, and often unrelated, varieties of shrubs, vines and trees that have fragrant white flowers

Jasmine perfumes are made from the flowers of several species, while Jasmine Tea is flavoured from Arabian Jasmine, which actually comes from SE Asia!.

Confederate (*Trachelospermum jasminoides*) and Chilean Jasmine (*Mandevilla laxa*) are in the Apocynaceae family; Night Blooming Jasmine (*Cestrum nocturnum*) is in the Solanaceae family; and South Carolina's state flower, Carolina Jasmine (*Gelsemium sempervirens*) is in the Loganiaceae family.

Jasmines can be found in the chapters on SHRUBS and VINES.

ALLAMANDA

Family: *Apocynaceae*

Allamanda cathartica

English: *Yellow Allamanda, Golden Trumpet, Buttercup Flower*

Spanish: *Alamanda, Canarias, Bejuco de San Jose*

Allamanda is native to Brazil and is very popular throughout Florida and the West Indies. It's classic deep yellow flowers identify this fast growing vine, 10-12ft. (3-3.6m), which basically blooms all the time. Run it on a fence, up a trellis, but always provide support as it has no tendrils for gripping. The foliage as well as the blooms are aromatic.

Allamanda vines are now seen in other colours besides yellow, including Chocolate Cream and Cherries Jubilee. There is also a shrub Allamanda—see the chapter on Shrubs.

Plant in full sun in most any decent soil. They have few pests, enjoy a little food, but are basically carefree. Normal water, propagate from cuttings or allow seed-heads to dry on plants, remove and collect seeds.

Danger: All parts of the plant are poisonous if ingested.

ANGELWING JASMINE

Family: *Oleaceae*

Jasminum nitidum

English: *Angelwing Jasmine, Shining Jasmine, Confederate Jasmine, Star Jasmine*

Spanish: *Jazmin*

Angelwing Jasmine is a wonderful vine with sweetly fragrant, snow-white, star shaped flowers, that start out as purple buds and retain some pinkish-purple on the calyx. They bloom at night from late spring through summer, fast growing, can reach heights of 20ft. (6m), or can be pruned into a small shrub.

Plant in light shade, average water, night bloomer, flowers in endless clusters, responds well to drastic pruning. Propagate from woody stem cuttings or from seed; sow indoors before last frost.

BLEEDING HEART

Family: *Verbenaceae*

Clerodendrum thomsoniae

English: *Bleeding Heart (Glorybower) Vine, Scarlet Kiss*

Spanish: *Arroz y Frijoles*

Another highly diverse genus that originates from West Africa, includes vines and shrubs. This romantic and beautiful vine will bloom all year in the right conditions. The name "Bleeding Heart Vine" is descriptive of its flowers which generally look like a red drop extending from the heart shaped bract, or, puckered red lips—Scarlet Kiss!

Able to withstand light freezes, though may be knocked down to the roots. Usually makes a fast recovery and will bloom the same year. Can also be grown as a rambling shrub, spreads by runners, but easily controlled. A good holder, after initial tying it can easily grow 6ft. (1.5m) in it's first year.

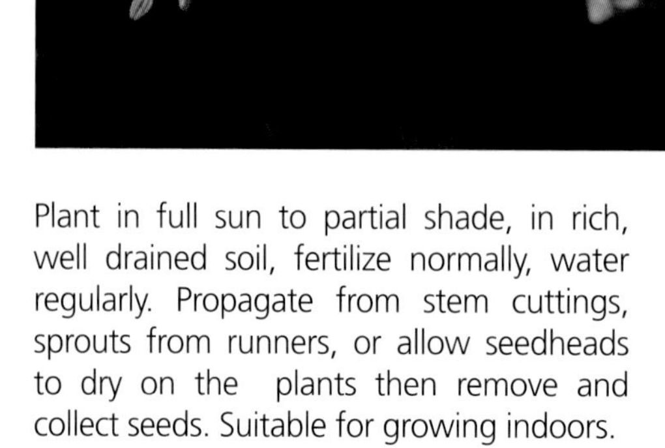

Plant in full sun to partial shade, in rich, well drained soil, fertilize normally, water regularly. Propagate from stem cuttings, sprouts from runners, or allow seedheads to dry on the plants then remove and collect seeds. Suitable for growing indoors.

English: *Bougainvillea, Paper Flower*

Spanish: *Buganvilea, Flor de Papel, Trinitaria, Napoleon*

BOUGAINVILLEA

Family: *Nyctaginaceae*

Genus: *Bougainvillea*

Named after French navigator Louis de Bougainville who discovered the bush while in Brazil, where the vine originates from. Also known as the 'paper flower' because of the flowers' delicate appearance, they bloom profusely throughout the Caribbean and southern United States.

Bougainvillea is prized for its intense colour with maximum colour in winter and spring.

The colour is not produced by the flowers but by the highly coloured bracts which most mistake as the flowers. Enclosed inside each "paper" case or bract is a single, tiny, tubular, white flower. Older vines produce better than younger individuals, there are many colours to choose from as well as dwarf and tree varieties.

They readily root from cuttings, show their best colours in 100% full sun, and can with-stand drought as well as heavy pruning. Minimum water. Wind protection is desirable. Do not tolerate salt spray well. This vine sprawls wildly and produces many stems from the ground. Plant over walls, over docks, on fences or in pots. A wonderful signature plant from the tropics.

Danger:
Very thorny, use gloves and caution when handling.

BOUGAINVILLEA TREE
Bougainvillea arborea

BOUGAINVILLEA TREE FLOWER
Bougainvillea arborea

CAPE HONEYSUCKLE

Family: *Bignoniaceae*

Tecomaria capensis

English: *Cape Honeysuckle*
Spanish: *Madreselva Capa*
Zulu: *Lungana, Uchahacha, Umunyane*

From South Africa, Cape Honeysuckle is a sprawling, rampant grower that provides dazzling colour to any garden, displaying bright orange-red to scarlet tubular flowers that bloom from late summer through winter. A hummingbird favorite. Considered a vine, it can be pruned to make a spectacular shrub reaching as high as10ft. (3m) and 25ft. (7.5m) long—a great fence cover.

Plant in full sun to partial shade, drought-tolerant, prune after flowering is done, propagate from cuttings, layering or dividing the rootball; seed collecting is difficult and not recommended.

English: *Cup of Gold, Chalice Vine, Golden Chalice*

Spanish: *Mendieta, Copa de Oro*

CHALICE VINE

Family: *Solanaceae*

Solandra grandiflora

A spectacular vine with blossoms up to 10inches (25cm) long, each bloom lasts for four days changing colour from cream to yellow gold to apricot orange before wilting off. A member of the potato family, native to the West Indies. The common Chalice Vine has very little fragrance while the variegated Chalice Vine has an intoxicating smell.

They make good container plants or dramatic large scale flowering vine outdoors; up to 60ft. (18m) in height. Can take full sun, blooms all year, can train over arbors and fences or up trees. Normal water and plant food, robust, fast grower.

Danger: All parts of this plant are poisonous if ingested.

CONFEDERATE JASMINE

Family: *Apocynaceae*

Trachelospermum jasminoides

English: *Confederate Jasmine, Star Jasmine*
Spanish: *Jazmin*

A native of China, Confederate Jasmine is a very popular ornamental in the southern US because it is very vigorous and has wonderfully scented flowers. A quick grower it can reach heights of 30-40ft. (9-12m), although around 20ft. (6m) is more common. It will grow to 6ft. (2m) or more in a pot.

Plant in full sun to partial shade, blooms from mid-spring to early summer, regular water, drought-tolerant, propagate from semi-hardwood cuttings.

Danger: All parts of this plant are poisonous if ingested. Handling plant may cause skin irritation. The plants contain an alkaloid that is much used in religious rituals of the Fang people of Gabon. It is also used in traditional Chinese medicine to lower blood pressure and dilate blood vessels, but an overdose can cause convulsions and respiratory arrest!

DUTCHMAN'S PIPE

Family: *Aristolochiaceae*

Aristolochia sp? Gigantea

nglish: *Dutchman's Pipe, Calico Vine, 'roadleafed Birthwort*

panish: *Algaria de Monte*

=rom this fascinating genus, with over 75 pecies, come many of the most unusual lowers in the world. From the side, the lowers often look like birds or resemble a Meerschaum pipe—"Dutchman's Pipes". Head on, many look like large maroon or green pouches that range from tiny 1 inch 2cm) to giant 12inch (30cm) monsters. For all the intricacies of their flowers, Aristolochias have no flower petals, just one fancy calyx.

The north American species have small pipe shaped, semi-fragrant, flowers while the south American species have huge flowers with the inner portion resembling calico fabric—hence Calico Vine.

The large blooms give off an aroma resembling rotten meat to attract the plant's key pollinators, insects and flies. Several species provide important food sources for butterfly larvae including the world's largest, the birdwing butterfly.

The blooms are a semi-trap in that insects arriving with pollen can only leave after the pollen exchange has taken place. The tube is lined with small downward pointing hairs that only relax if it detects the new pollen, thus allowing the insect out.

Easy to grow, fast climbers, 20-30ft. (6-9m), fine in full sun to partial shade, can be grown in pots, average water, propagate from stem cuttings or divide the rootball. Plant seeds in the autumn. Essential for any butterfly garden.

Danger: Aristolochia are also called Birthworts and as such turn up in herbal medicine to ease the pain of childbirth to treating malaria. However parts of plant are highly toxic if ingested especially to the kidneys. Incorrect doses can cause vomiting, pain and even death. Any homemade medication using Aristolochia should be avoided completely.

FRANGAPANI VINE

Family: *Apocynaceae*

Chonemorpha fragrans

English: *Frangipani Vine, Climbing Frangipan*
Spanish: *Franchipán, Franchipán de Vid*

This beautiful woody climber with it's large shiny green leaves and fragrant ornamental flowers originates in the forests of India and Malaya, where it can be observed growing to the tops of the trees.

Latex bearing, Frangipani Vine has also been used in traditional medicine for centuries while modern scientists have isolated steroid properties in the plant.

Plant in full sun to partial shade, regular water, acidic soil preferred, will reach 10ft. (3m) but can climb entire tree in the wild, fragrant white propeller flowers, blooms late spring into mid-summer, attracts butterflies and hummingbirds, somewhat cold tolerant, can survive mild frost for short periods.

nglish: *Mexican Creeper, Coral Vine,* *oves Chain*

panish: *Coralillo, Rosa de Montana,* *Cadena del Amor, Bellisima*

MEXICAN CREEPER

Family: *Polygonaceae*

Antigonon leptopus

Coral vine is related to the Florida sea grape and is native to Tropical and Latin America (Mexico). It is a favorite for its showy flowers, like strings of small pink hearts, seen mostly in summer and autumn, but can have some blooms anytime.

Plant in full sun in most any soil, water to establish, will grow to 40ft. (12m), prune to control, drought tolerant, propagate by seeds or 'volunteer' plants, attractive to bees, birds and butterflies. Coral vine climbs on tendrils so fences to palm trees are excellent bases. Also light pink and white varieties. This is a carefree vine to own.

MORNING GLORY

Family: *Convolvulaceae*

Genus: *Ipomoea*

English: *Morning Glory*

Spanish: *Campana*

Native to the tropics, more than 200 species of Morning Glories come from the Americas alone. They boast showy trumpet shaped flowers ranging from light blue to rose, mauve, violet, lavender, plus white and multi-coloured, that can be up to 8inches (20cm) across; with 3-4inches (7-10cm) more common. Morning Glories bloom continually from summer through autumn, each flower opens in the morning and lasts for one day.

Morning glory vines grow very fast, reaching 10ft. (3m) or more, two months after seeds sprout, and they will climb on just about any support. The vines are sometimes used as a temporary ground cover, and do well in hanging baskets and containers. This plant is attractive to bees, butterflies and birds.

Plant in full sun to partial shade and need a soil that is not too fertile or moist to prevent the production of leaves instead of flowers. Normal water, propagate with tubers or rooted cuttings, soak or nick seeds before planting. From seed; sow indoors before last frost and outdoors direct sow after last frost.

Danger: Parts of this plant are poisonous if ingested.

MORNING GLORY FLOWER

ORANGE TRUMPET VINE

Family: *Bignoniaceae*

Pyrostegia venusta

English: *Orange Trumpet Vine, Flame Vine, Golden Shower*

Spanish: *Lluvia de Oro*

The flame vine from Brazil is a rampant growing climber that requires full sun. Able to cover very large areas with glorious colour. Its powerful growth means the owner has to be watchful—it is best to prune your vine back hard after the blooming season. The vine blooms in later winter and into the spring in South Florida.

Plant in full sun to partial shade into plain sandy soil but enriched with organic matter.

Water to establish then there is little else to do but enjoy. Use flame vine where you want quick, thorough coverage; will reach to 40ft. (12m), propagate from semi-hardwood cuttings. Blazing colour and spectacular.

English: *Passion Vine, Passion Flower, Grenadilla*

Spanish: *Granadilla, Pasaflora, Maracuya*

PASSION VINES

Family: *Passifloraceae*

Genus: *Passiflora*

Passion vines now number over 600 species with more hybrids on the way, and are native to tropical America in places like Brazil, Venezuela, Mexico and Peru. Depending on variety, bold and striking flowers varying from a 1/2inch (1cm) to as much as 6inches (15cm) across appear in spring through to autumn. Violet, lavender and reds predominate.

Many Passiflora have very complex flowers, some are scented, some are used in commercial perfumes, and in the early 1600's Catholic priests in Peru saw a religious symbolism to this plant. The name "passion flower" is said to derive from the vine's flower resembling the crown of thorns placed on Christ's head. Others say that the parts of the plant symbolize features of the Crucifixion, known as *The Passion of Christ*. The ten sepals and petals are the ten apostles (minus Judas and Peter), the darker circle the crown of thorns, the five stamens the wound, the three styles the nails, and the leaves the hands of the persecutors.

A famous member is the *Passiflora edulis* which produces attractive purple flowers and edible fruit. The fruit is fairly seedy but the squeezed juice is a tropical delight —Grenadilla!

Passion vines are good climbers using their tendrils to wrap around any support. They grow quickly, as much as 15-20ft. (4-8m) or more per season. Plant in full sun to partial shade, average water do not overwater, propagate from cuttings or layering.

RED PASSION FLOWER
Passiflora coccinea

GRENADILLA
Passiflora edulis

English: *Queen's Wreath, Purple Wreath, Bluebird Vine, Sandpaper Vine, Lilac*

Spanish: *Petrea, Chaparro*

PETREA

Family: *Verbenaceae*

Petrea volubilis

This wonderful vine, endemic to Central America, is spectacular in bloom with cascades of blue-violet flowers. The flowers only last a few days, but the calices stay longer and turn grey-violet, then serve as the wings for the seeds. There is also a small tree, *Petrea arborea*, much like the vine with the same profuse sprays of flowers; as well as a white variety, *Petrea kohautiana*—or Bridal Wreath.

Plant in full sun to partial shade, average water, easy to maintain, will grow to a height of 30-40ft. (9-12m). Be sure to prune this vine after blooming to encourage another show. Propagate with cuttings or from seed, sow indoors before last frost and outdoors direct sow after last frost. Blooms from late winter through early autumn, a favorite of bees and butterflies. Great for beginner gardeners!

RANGOON CREEPER

Family: *Combretaceae*

Quisqualis indica

English: *Rangoon Creeper, Drunken Sailor, Akar Dani*

Spanish: *Enredadera de Rangoon, Cocuisa (DR)*

Originating in tropical Asia from New Guinea to China this fast growing splendid vine has wonderful fragrant (especially at night) blooms that start out white and mature through pink to red. There is also a double flower variety available; *Quisqualis indica* "Double".

Considered an astringent plant, the bark, seed and leaves are all used in traditional medicine, with each black fruit containing a single seed.

Ideal fast grower for any garden the plant needs support from fences, a trellis or walls.

Plant in full sun to partial shade, average water, will reach 40ft.+ (12m), observed to 70ft. (21m) in the wild. Blooms late spring through mid-autumn, will handle short freezes if protected, propagate from seed, direct sow in autumn or root cuttings, good container plant, should be trimmed annually after flowering, may be considered a noxious weed or invasive in some areas.

English: *Thunbergia, Bengal Trumpet, Sky Flower, Bengal Clock Vine, Blue Sky Vine*

Spanish: *Fausto*

THUNBERGIA

Family: *Acanthaceae*

Thunbergia grandiflora

From Africa and India this very showy vine with wonderful blue flowers will thrive practically anywhere, and blooms almost continually. Similar to the Morning Glory vine. It rambles and will grow 15-20ft. (4–7.6m), in a single season, so expect to prune.

Plant in full sun to partial shade, normal fertilizer and water. Propagate by dividing the rootball or from leaf and stem cuttings. You can also allow seedheads to dry on plants then remove and collect seeds. Growth slows or stops in cool temperatures, and the top is killed to the ground after a freeze. Blooms can also be violet, lavender or white.

THUNBERGIA & RED PASSION VINE

AMERICAN WISTERIA

Family: *Fabaceae*

Wisteria frutescens

English: *American Wisteria, Kentucky Wisteria*
Spanish: *Vid de Americano*

Wisteria is named after Caspar Wistar, an 18th century American professor of anatomy. This is the Native American Wisteria, which is much less commonly used in gardens in the US than Chinese and Japanese Wisteria, which are traditional bonsai subjects.

The wisteria is known for the beauty of its spectacular flower shows, which appear in long, 6-12inch (15-30cm), cascading racemes that are blue-violet to violet-lavender. Wild American Wisteria covers the US southeast in mid-spring with a dazzling and fragrant display; an artist and photographer's delight.

Once established, (generally at about five years of age), very rapid growth rate occurs, maturing at 30ft. (10m) or more. Plant in full sun to partial shade, average water, suitable for growing indoors. Propagate by rooted stem cuttings or seeds. A woody vine it can be pruned into a shrub or small tree. Grows over everything —watch out!

Danger. All parts of plant including the seeds are poisonous if ingested. Do not allow children or animals to ingest them.

English: *Woolly Morning Glory, Woodrose, Silver Elephant Creeper, Baby Woodrose, Baby Hawaiian Woodrose, Cordon Seda, Coup D'Air, Elephant Creeper*

Spanish: *Vid de Campana*

WOOLLY MORNING GLORY

Family: *Convolvulaceae*

Argyreia speciosa

This family of 55 genera comprises some 1650 species of herbs, shrubs or trees, many of which are climbing. They are found in tropical and temperate regions. From India, Woolly Morning Glory is most popular for it's huge contrasting silver and green leaves and purported medicinal properties.

In Hindu medicine, the plant is deemed a valuable general antiseptic. The leaves are used in native medicine as poultices, the roots and seeds as a support of the nervous system, a geriatric tonic and mild aphrodisiac. The whole plant is reported to have purifying properties, maintain healthy joints and several have purgative properties and are the sources of drugs used in medicine.

Plant in sun to partial shade, average water, will reach 30-40ft. (9-12m), blooms repeatedly, propagate from hardwood cuttings or from seed, direct sow after last frost. Seed collecting, allow seedheads to dry on plants then remove and collect seeds. Easy to grow, may be considered a noxious weed or invasive by some.

ROYAL POINCIANA GARDEN – SOUTH FLORIDA

Chapter 11
Trees

The visual identity of nature in the tropics, tropical trees are just fabulous, providing gifts to mankind throughout the ages.

Homes, protection and shelter, medicine, utensils, transportation, weapons, warmth, food, furniture to rope, fragrance, shade and above all colour and beauty, are every-day gifts from these glorious plants.

For home landscaping observe what grows well in your area, visit local botanical gardens and nurseries and of course do some research on not only the tree's requirements but also it's final size, maintenance, foliage, blooming and fruiting patterns. Trees can be vital in reducing home bills by providing shade along with privacy, beauty and value to your property. They provide homes for wildlife and oxygen for the air your breath.

When choosing large trees you must consider your neighbours, consult with them and the resulting cooperation can be mutually beneficial in terms of shade, produce and privacy.

One should always notice and appreciate tropical trees, always make an effort to protect them, and always make an effort to plant more.

English: *African Tulip Tree, Flame of the Forest, Fountain Tree*

Spanish: *Tulipán Africano, Arbol de Fuente, Espatodea, Llamarada de Bosque*

AFRICAN TULIP TREE

Family: *Bignoniaceae*

Spathodea campanulata

Originally from Equatorial Africa the African Tulip Tree is a spectacular flowering tree and is famous throughout the tropical world. Related to Jacaranda and Tabebuia, it grows as wide as it grows tall producing an immense shade canopy. It has naturalized in many parts of the Indo-Pacific where it can be considered an invasive. However it's outrageous flowers are a huge attraction.

The unopened buds contain water which squirt when squeezed or pierced. After blooming, large pods are grown which later release winged seeds. The bark and leaves are used in traditional medicine, the soft, white timber used in making paper, drums and blacksmith's bellows.

A fast growing tropical ornamental, plant in full sun, moist rich soil, will reach 80ft. (24m), everblooming, propagate from seeds, root suckers and cuttings. Attractive to birds and bats Widely grown in gardens where there is no frost. Weak branches will break in a hurricane.

ANGEL'S TRUMPET TREE

Family: *Solanaceae*

Datura candida or Brugmansia candida

English: *Angel's Trumpet Tree, Daturas, Angel's Tears*

Spanish: *Campana*

Daturas are in the Nightshade family (Solanaceae), native to Brazil or possibly the mountains of Chile and Peru—there are about 20 different species and hundreds of cultivars ranging from annual and perennial herbs to shrubs and trees, with fabulous trumpet-shaped flowers. Nearly all are poisonous and all are hallucinogenic. Natives in Brazil smoke the leaves for a strong narcotic effect said to relieve asthma! In many parts of the world these plants are still a source of pharmaceutical tropane alkaloids such as scopolamine and atropine.

Most are intoxicatingly fragrant at night!

Plant in full sun to partial shade, the more sun the more flowers. Will reach 15-18ft. (4.5-5.5m). Can be pruned into a nice small striking garden ornamental. Blooms on and off all year. Easy to grow. Not fussy about soil or water. Likes lots of fertilizer. Easy to keep in large pots and bring into the house for the winter. Flowers are fragrant, attractive to bees and butterflies, propagate from leaf, stem or softwood cuttings. Seed collecting, allow seedheads to dry on plants then remove and collect seeds.

Danger: All parts of plant are poisonous if ingested. Whole plant contains a strong narcotic.

AUTOGRAPH TREE

Family: *Clusiaceae*

Clusia rosea

English: *Autograph Tree, Pitch Apple, Balsam Apple, Scotch Attorney, Copey, Balsam Fig*

Spanish: *Cupey, Matapalo, Tampaco, Cape, Cucharo, Chuchi Copei*

These beautiful and interesting evergreen trees with their huge top spreads make fabulous shade trees in the hottest climates. A West Indian native it is common in all tropical areas and widely grown as an ornamental, street or parking lot tree. It can germinate in the crotch of other trees, grow as an epiphyte, and send down aerial roots that will eventually smother the host tree.

The thick, large ovate leaves are it's namesake as they are reputed to have been used by Spanish conquistadors as both playing cards and writing paper. Certainly any words scratched onto the leaf remain there permanently, while along with the fruit and bark are also used in home medicines. The large seed pods (3inches or 8cm) turn from green to brown and split revealing black seeds in red flesh.

Plant in full sun to partial shade, most any soil, can reach 50ft. (15m) with spreads to 30ft. (9m), moderate water needs, salt and drought tolerant, suitable for xeriscaping, blooms in summer, large white fragrant flowers followed by woody fruit, propagate by seed and cuttings. Attractive to bees and fruit eating birds. Low maintenance, can be container grown.

Danger: Parts of the plant are poisonous if ingested plus handling may cause skin irritation or allergic reaction—wear gloves when handling.

AUTOGRAPH TREE
Clusia rosea

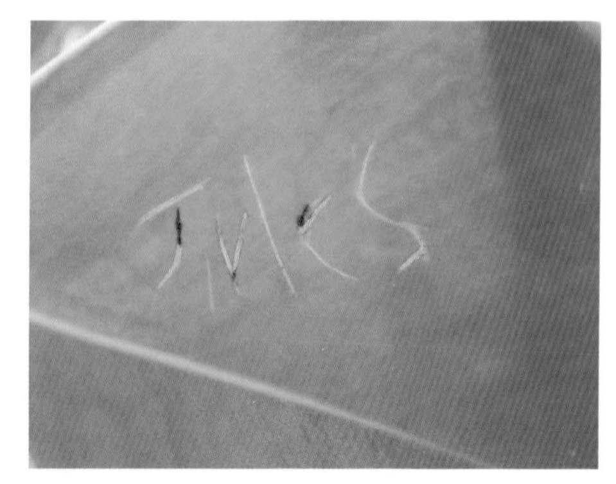

English: *Bottlebrush Tree, Weeping Bottlebrush*
Spanish: *Calistemon*

BOTTLEBRUSH TREE

Family: *Myrtaceae*
Callistemon viminalis

The beautiful family that is bottlebrushes are about 25-30 species of shrubs and trees native to Australia and New Caledonia, with numerous varieties and cultivars with fabulous names like, Texas, Little John, Captain Cook, and Dawson River Weeper. They grow easily in tropical and semi-tropical climates and their amazing bright red bottle-brush shaped flowers bloom off and on throughout the hot weather. The floral parts are greatly reduced except for the numerous long stamens, giving the flowers their signature bottlebrush design, and Latin identification; Callistemon, from the Greek "*kalos*", meaning beautiful and "*stemon*", meaning stamens—beautiful stamens; viminalis...from the Latin "*viminalis*", with long flexible twigs.

Plant in full sun, will reach up to 30ft. (9m) – to 60ft. (18m) in native Australia, like well drained soil, drought-tolerant, suitable for xeriscaping, attractive to hummingbirds, butterflies and bees. Propagate from seed and cuttings. Named cultivars must be propagated from cuttings due to genetic variation that occurs in seedlings. Read up on seed development, harvesting and planting - easier to buy from local nursery! Related to the Paper Bark or Cajetput-tree.

CALABASH TREE

Family: *Bignoniaceae*

Crescentia cujete

English: *Mexican Calabash Tree, Calabash Tree*

Spanish: *Calabasa, Cujete, Higüero, Güira, Guaje, Morro, Guacal, Totumo, Calabazo, Arbol de las Calabazas*

Found growing throughout the Caribbean, Mexico, Central America, and northern South America the exact origin of the Calabash Tree is blurred by history. This multi-purpose highly useful tree was used for centuries by native populations.

The Taíno of the Caribbean are reputed to have used them as hunting aids, cutting eyeholes and placing over their heads they then entered the water and quietly stalked waterfowl who were unperturbed by "floating gourds".

Tree fibres were twisted into twine and ropes, the hard wood into tools, while split into strips to weave large sturdy baskets.

However the oval hard shelled fruit is the centre piece of it's claim to fame. Dried calabashes have and are still used as bowls,

Band - SEXTETO CLAVE SOL.
Old Havana, Cuba

storage containers, dippers, drinking cups, decoration and painted for tourist souvenirs. They can be trained into different shapes by tying when green, woven with grass handles to carry water, or have ornamental value in home decoration.

The Taíno also gave the musical world two rhythm instruments, the maracas and the güiro. Original maracas were made from a calabash gourd with hard seeds inside, while the güiro was an elongated gourd that has carved ribbing that a player runs a stick up and down to create the sound.

Native populations did not survive European diseases but their legacy lives on in music with Mexico being synonymous with the maracas and Puerto Rico identified with the güiro.

Plant in full sun, will reach 30ft. (9m), can have multiple trunks, night bloomer, blooms late spring through mid winter, pollinated by bats, large non-edible woody fruit (12inches or 30cm) takes 6-7 months to ripen, will survive short frosts, propagate by seed, low maintenance.

CANNONBALL TREE

Family: *Lecythidaceae*

Couroupita guianensis

English: *Cannonball Tree, Carrion Tree*

Spanish: *Bala de Cañón, Coco de Mono, Moke Muco*

Believed to be a native to the rainforests of the Guiana's in northeastern South America, this outrageous tree is a delight and novelty wherever it grows. Pollinated by bats, the amazing flowers, used in perfumes and cosmetics, are heavenly scented and are formed off unusual thick woody extensions that grow from the main trunk and cascade down in large numbers. It's name obviously derives from the large brown fruit balls in the size and shape of rusty cannonballs that dangle from fruit branches. The fruit contains small seeds in a white, unpleasant smelling jelly.

Plant in full sun to partial shade, moist soil, needs high humidity and likes water. Can reach 75ft. (23m), flowers—followed by fruit, grow directly from the trunk. Fruits are soft and very fleshy, propagate from seed. Very susceptible to frost, so plant in frost free locations. The fruit is edible but the aroma usually discourages all but the hardy. The hard fruit shells can be used as containers.

CANNONBALL TREE FLOWERS

CREPE MYRTLE

Family: *Lythraceae*

Lagerstroemia indica

English: *Crepe Myrtle, Crape Myrtle*

Spanish: *Jupiter, Astromelia, Astromero*

From China and Korea this genus of some 50 species was introduced into cultivation in 1747 and named for the Swedish merchant Magnus von Lagerstrom. One of the splendor trees of summer and an icon of the Southeastern US landscape, Crepes are grown for their striking crepe-paperlike blooms in shades of white, pink, lavender and red. Crepe Myrtles look fresh even on the hottest day and provide low-maintenance flowers on multi-trunked small trees. The silvery bark peels, revealing shades of brown and gray, while it's foliage matures from a reddish-bronze to green, with red or yellow autumn colours. A winner.

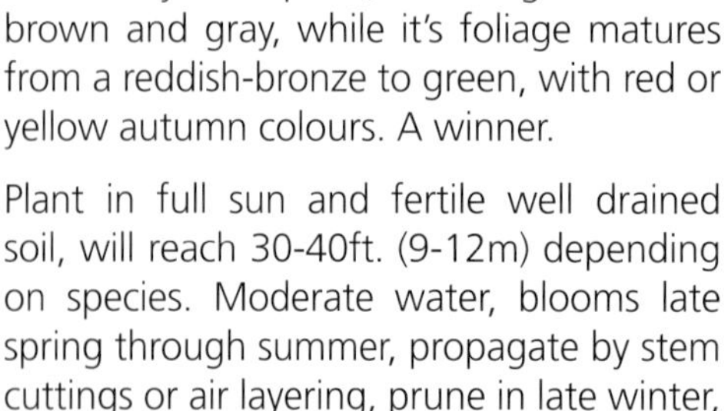

Plant in full sun and fertile well drained soil, will reach 30-40ft. (9-12m) depending on species. Moderate water, blooms late spring through summer, propagate by stem cuttings or air layering, prune in late winter, can be used in bonsai and as cut flowers.

DWARF POINCIANA

Family: *Fabaceae*

Caesalpinia pulcherrima

Poinciana pulcherrima

English: *Dwarf Poinciana, Pride of Barbados, Red Bird of Paradise, Peacock Flower*

Spanish: *Framboyán Francés, Guacamaya*

National flower of Barbados.

Aptly named, *Caesalpinia pulcherrima— "the most beautiful Caesalpinia"*—this small, graceful tree flowers throughout the year and is a beautiful garden plant, a showy miniature of the Royal Poinciana. Of vague origin, from northwestern South America through Central America and the West Indies, it's flower is actually the sacred flower of Siva in India. The stem and branches are armed with spines. The red, orange, yellow and pink flowers grow at the end of the prickly branches. The fruits are legumes, 3-4inches (8-10cm), when ripe they split open and release the brown bean.

Plant in full sun to partial shade, average to low water, suitable for xeriscaping, will reach 15ft. (4.5m), blooms almost all year round, best summer through autumn. Attractive to bees, butterflies and humming-birds, self-sows freely, so deadhead if you do not want volunteer seedlings next season. Propagate from seed, direct sow after last frost. Seed collecting, bag seedheads to capture ripening seed and allow pods to dry on plant then break open to collect seeds.

Danger: The seed and parts of the plant are poisonous if ingested.

English: *Frangipani, Pagoda Tree, Temple Tree, Plumeria*

Spanish: *Franchipán, Lirio de la Costa, Aleli, Amapola*

FRANGIPANI

Family: *Apocynaceae*

Plumeria spp.

Treasured by Polynesian islanders for their durability, fragrance and colours of whites, yellows, pinks, reds, and multiple pastels, there's nothing quite like nature's fragrance of Plumeria in bloom. Flowering can last up to 3 months at a time producing new blooms everyday. Once picked, if kept in water, a bloom can last for several days without wilting.

Native to warm tropical areas of the Pacific Islands, Caribbean, South America and Mexico, Plumeria is the classic Hawaiian lei tree. Its flowers are the ones used to form the colourful, tropical flower necklaces—lei! It is often planted in and near temples and graveyards in Sri Lanka, East and West Indies & Hawaii—hence Temple Tree. There are well over 130 different cultivars and varieties that include both trees and shrubs. Gorgeous.

Plant in full sun to shifting shade, water deeply but infrequently, depending on species will reach from 8-40ft. (2.5-12m), bloom late spring into early autumn, propagate from cuttings or seed—sow indoors before last frost. Seed collecting, allow seedheads to dry on plants then remove and collect seeds. Frangipani is deciduous losing all its leaves in winter looking a bit scrappy in it's dormant stage—this is normal. Make great cut flowers, good container plant. Winter indoors in cold climates.

GEIGER TREES

Family: *Boraginaceae*

Cordia sebestena

English: *Geiger Tree, Cordia, Geranium Tree, Anaconda*

Spanish: *Vomitel, Cutiperi, San Bartoleme, Capa*

Audubon himself was in Key West in 1832 drawing and painting when he noted two unusual trees; 'Both trees were on private property, and grew in a yard opposite to that of Dr. Strobel,' he wrote. Historians using Key West records have been able to document that Dr. Strobel's neighbor was a Captain Geiger, Key West's first Harbour Pilot who made his fortune as a wrecking master salvaging ships that foundered on the treacherous reefs.

The Cordia tree, now named Geiger, thus became part of Key's history. Native to the Caribbean basin, there is also White (*Cordia boissieri*), Yellow (*Cordia lutea*) and Brazilian (*Cordia superba*) along with some 200 further species of the genus Cordia.

Easy to grow, plant in full sun to partial shade, regular water, drought tolerant, will reach 25ft. (7.5m), blooms all year, propagate from seed direct sow after last frost. Bears small, fragrant fruit, edible but lack flavour.

YELLOW GEIGER
Cordia lutea

YELLOW GEIGER FLOWERS
Cordia lutea

GOLDEN RAIN TREE

Family: *Sapindaceae*

Koelreuteria paniculata

English: *Golden Rain Tree, Varnish Tree*
Spanish: *Arbol de Aureo Lluvia, Arbol de Barn*

This beautiful native from China puts on an amazing show, the large pinnate leaves emerge hot pink in spring before turning a rich green, large panicles of fragrant bright yellow flowers follow through the summer, followed by fascinating pink or red-flushed fruit capsules, paper lantern-like, in the autumn. The fallen blossoms form a romantic golden carpet beneath the tree.

Plant in full sun, fast grower, average water, will reach 40ft. (12m), tolerates city conditions, propagate from seed and root cuttings, blooms summer through autumn. Thrives almost everywhere, takes the cold, heat, drought and wind well. May need pruning to help keep shape. Seed collecting, allow pods to dry on plant then break open to collect seeds. Properly cleaned, seed can be successfully stored. Considered a shade tree. Listed as an invasive in Florida.

English: *Golden Shower Tree, Cassia, Pudding Pipe Tree, Purging Cassia, Golden Chain Tree, Indian Laburnum*

Spanish: *Cañafístola*

GOLDEN SHOWER TREE

Family: *Fabaceae*

Cassia fistula

Cassia is a huge genus, with about 500 species, that includes many of the most colourful trees and shrubs in the tropics, and to many, the finest Cassia is the fistula. Native to South Asia and especially India where it's long, up to 3ft. (90cm), black pods give it the name Pudding Pipe, and purgative qualities the Purging Cassia, it's flower show is something special. Widely planted as a handsome ornamental tree, the reddish wood, hard and heavy, strong and durable, is suited for cabinetwork, farm implements, inlay work, posts, wheels, mortars, etc. The bark has been employed in tanning, while the drug "*cassia fistula*", a laxative, is obtained from the sweetish sticky brown pulp around the seed. Cassia fistula is used world wide in traditional medicines, especially as a purgative.

Easy to grow, plant in full sun for best flowering, average water, tolerant of many soils and light salt drift, will reach 30-40ft. (9-12m), fantastic fragrant bright yellow flowers, blooms late spring through mid summer, attractive to bees and butterflies, propagate from seed. Study-up on seed collecting, storage and growing. Happy, popular, colourful.

Danger: All parts of plant are poisonous if ingested, large doses can cause vomiting, nausea, abdominal pain and severe cramps.

GOLDEN TRUMPET TREE

Family: *Bignoniaceae*

Tabebuia caraiba

English: *Golden Trumpet Tree, Yellow Tabebuia, Silver Trumpet Tree, Caribbean Trumpet Tree, Silver Tabebuia*

Spanish: *Cortés, Guayacán Amarillo, Guayacán, Hahauche*

Multiple Latin synonyms and common names.

The Tabebuia are trumpet trees, for their trumpet shaped flowers, with over 150 species, that come from the West Indies, South and Central America. The genus name Tabebuia is a modification of "*tacyba bebuya*", an old Brazilian Indian name.

The Golden or Silver Trumpet tree is a native of Brazil, related to the flame vine and jacaranda tree, and is considered by many as one of the most beautiful flowering trees in the world.

The "Silver" comes from the synonym argentea and also the silver grey bark and branches, whose contorted trunks give year round visual appeal.

Plant in partial to full sun, average water, will reach 30-40ft. (9-12m), once established drought tolerant, blooms late winter through early spring, propagate from air layering or seed. Seed collecting, allow seedheads to dry on plants then remove and collect seeds Seed does not store well, direct sow as soon as possible after last frost. Easy to grow, no pests, low maintenance, beautiful flowering tree. Can be container grown. Outstanding small trees well suited for residential plantings. Highly regarded as street trees in Florida.

English: *Jacaranda, Fern Tree, Bignonia, Blue Jacaranda*

Spanish: *Framboyán Azul, Jacarandá, Palo de Buba*

JACARANDA

Family: *Bignoniaceae*

Jacaranda mimosifolia

One of nature's most impressive sites is a row of Jacarandas in bloom. Native to South America and the Caribbean basin about 50 tropical and subtropical species of trees and shrubs are world renowned for their fabulous intense blue flower displays which can last up to two months. The ground beneath them also turns into a peaceful violet blue carpet of nature. A deciduous ornamental

Jacaranda is good for urban, street and boulevard plantings. When not in bloom, the trees can be hard to tell from Royal Poinciana and produce a wonderful broken shade during the hot months.

Plant in full sun and well drained soil, likes moisture, will reach (depending on species) from 25-50-ft. (7.5-15m), drought tolerant, blooms early spring to early summer. Stunning flowers in blues, violets, lavenders and purples—yellow and white variations, cultivars available. Propagate from cuttings or seed, direct sow outdoors in autumn. Seed collecting, allow pods to dry on plant then break open to collect seeds. Grow for beauty and summer shade.

LIGNUM VITAE

Family: *Zygophyllaceae*

Guaiacum officinale

From the Latin lignum vitae for *"wood of life"* this extraordinary tree is indigenous to tropical America and the West Indies, was "discovered" by Columbus, and has been in high demand for centuries. The body, gum/resin, bark, fruit, leaves and flowers are all used in various ways leading to overexploitation throughout the species' range which now results in it's endangerment—less than 2500 mature individuals exit naturally and is now extinct on several island nations.

Guaiacum comes from the Caribe for "medicine gum" the sap was used for treating everything from syphilis (combined with mercury) to gout, as a purgative and other various ailments!

Extremely dense, heaviest of all commercial woods, will sink in water, was used in a huge range of items such as mortars, mallets, pulleys, police batons, carvings, judges' gavels, and at one time as wooden propeller shaft bearings, as it's high resin content makes it self lubricating, in nearly every wood vessel upon the seas.

English: *Lignum Vitae, Tree of Life, Guaiacum, Guayacan, Pockholz*

Spanish: *Guayacán, Palo Santo, Guayacán de Playa, Guayaco, Arbol la Vida*

National flower of Jamaica.

Plant in full sun, average water, will reach 20-30ft. (6-9m) even to 40ft. (12m), once established salt and drought-tolerant, suitable for xeriscaping, blooms late spring, propagate from seed—scarify seed before sowing. Slow grower in the wild, faster if cultivated. Extremely ornamental, producing an attractive blue flower and orange-yellow fruit. Used in bonsai. Five species in the family. Protected in Florida. World trade regulated.

English: *Long John Tree, Mulatto Tree, Ant Tree*

Spanish: *Tachí, Barrabas, Palo María, Volador, Hormigo*

LONG JOHN TREE

Family: *Polygonaceae*

Triplaris americana

Native from northern South America to Panama, the amazing Mulatto tree is a deciduous tropical growing up to100ft.+ (30m+) and is called Long John because it is slender, tall and graceful. In Brazil and Venezuela it's called "*Tachi*" after the ant that eats out the centre of the tree, hence Ant Tree. In Suriname it is also called "drei tin" or dry time, which reminds one that when it blooms, the dry season is about to start.

Plant in full sun, average water, well drained soil or sandy loam, can tolerate some drought, will reach 100ft.+ (30m+), flowers in great panicles, very long leaves 1ft. (30cm), propagate from seed. A handsome ornamental flowering tree. Considered an invasive in some countries, especially South Africa.

The small white flowers are in big compound clusters, turn pink in their prime and finally brown. Enlarged calyces grow after the petals dry and are more ornamental, blazing red, than the flowers, develop into conspicuous wings adhering to the fruit, small square nuts, and the fruit falls with a spinning helicopter motion due to the calyx wings.

MELALEUCA or PAPERBARK TREE

Family: *Myrtaceae*

Melaleuca quinquenervia

English: *Melaleuca, White Bottlebrush Tree, Punk Tree, Australian Paperbark Tree, Cajeput Tree, Broadleaved Paperbark*

Spanish: *Melaleuca*

A native of Australia, New Guinea and New Caledonia the White Bottlebrush Tree was introduced to South Florida in aerial seeding in the 1930's to drain the swamps and Everglades for development and farmland —what a huge mistake. It has taken over hundreds of thousand of acres choking out important native plants that provide food and shelter for wildlife in Florida's ecosystems and represents a severe threat to the integrity of the Florida Everglades. Melaleuca contains Cajeput oil which is strongly antiseptic, has many medicinal uses, and is big in aromatherapy. The oil is usually harvested from *Melaleuca leucadendron*, which are grown commercially in Australia and the East Indies.

Plant in full sun to light shade, will reach up to 100ft. (30m), needs enough water to bloom well, tolerates poor drainage, dislikes drought, fast grower, wind and salt tolerant, blooms repeatedly, attractive to bees, butterflies and birds, propagate from both seed and cuttings - easy, will self-sow freely. A single tree can produce 20 million seeds per year.

Danger: Melaleuca flower pollen can cause respiratory irritation, headache and nausea. Contact with the bark can cause a skin rash.

Warning: Melaleuca is on Florida's official list of noxious plants, and its cultivation and possession are prohibited by state law. It is not allowed for importation to the US, nor is it allowed in any interstate transportation without a specific permit by the USDA.

English: *Mimosa, Silk Tree, Pink Siris*
Spanish: *Mimosa, Arbol de Seda*

MIMOSA

Family: *Fabaceae*

Albizia julibrissin

From a natural habitat range that spreads from Iran east across northern India, through Nepal, China and to Japan, the Mimosa or Silk Tree is a beautiful deciduous whose fuzzy pink, fragrant flower display is not only a summer delight, but can also reach shade spreads of 60ft. (18m).

Each fernlike bipinnate leaf is made up of hundreds of tiny leaflets which close up at night. The flowers are shed during the summer with the leaflets and seed pods each autumn, which can create an over abundance of self seeding and extra maintenance. Best to grow along fence lines, roadsides, fields and highways. From homeowners to impressionist painters many people call the Mimosa the most beautiful tree in the world

Plant in sun to partial shade, average water, once established is drought tolerant, fast grower, will reach 30-40ft. (9-12m), summer bloomer, attractive to bees, butterflies and hummingbirds, propagate from seed—direct sow outdoors in autumn. Seed collecting, allow pods to dry on plant then break open to collect seeds. May be considered a noxious weed or invasive. Cultivars: Charlotte and Tryon are disease resistant. Beautiful tree.

Danger: Pollen may cause allergic reaction.

OCTOPUS TREE

Family: *Araliaceae*

Schefflera actinophylla

English: *Octopus Tree, Queensland Umbrella Tree, Schefflera*

Spanish: *Cheflera, Arbol de Pulpo*

Native to Australia, New Guinea and Java, the Umbrella or Octopus Tree is very common in South Florida and the warmer parts of Central Florida. In fact an easy grower and self-starter considered by some as a nuisance for it's destructive root system, messy leaves and invasive qualities.

Observers in New Guinea report seeing Schefflera growing epiphytically starting as much as 40ft. (12m) up in tall rainforest trees. There are numerous dwarf and variegated varieties, very popular in Hawaii, make great potted and indoor plants.

Plant in partial shade, average water, unless potted can reach 40ft. (12m), can take heavy pruning, flowers bloom mid-summer through early autumn, propagate from seed or hardwood cuttings. The deep red flowers occur in long racemes from the top of the foliage and it is not unusual for 20 or more racemes to develop from each branch. The flowers are attractive to honey-eating birds and the fleshy fruits are attractive to fruit-eating birds.

English: *Orchid Tree, Butterfly Tree, Ox or Bull-Hoof, Napoleon's Hat*

Spanish: *Palo de Orquideas, Urape, Casco de Buey*

ORCHID TREES

Family: *Fabaceae*

One of the finest flowering trees in the tropics, Orchid trees are native to northern India through Vietnam and into south-eastern China. There are over 300 species and cultivars with many being shrubs and small trees. Wonderfully beautiful when in bloom, whole trees are covered with spectacular and fragrant orchid-like blossoms in shades of white, pink, purple, magenta and even red or yellow.

A deciduous whose leaves are shaped like the footprint of an ox or bull—hence "Bull-Hoof". The most famous of the species is the Hong Kong Orchid Tree, a sterile hybrid, producing extra large, deep purple, scented flowers in winter.

PURPLE ORCHID TREE
Bauhinia purpurea

Plant in full sun to partial shade, enriched soil, good drainage, average water, fast grower, will reach 20-30ft. (6-9m), requires proper feeding to have nice leaves, aromatic, attracts hummingbirds and butterflies, blooms late winter through summer, propagate from seed. Seed collecting, allow to dry on plants then remove, does not store well so plant promptly. May be considered a noxious weed or invasive in some areas.

Note: according to the USDA Bauhinias are in the Fabaceae family not the Caesalpiniaceae family.

MOUNTAIN EBONY
Bauhinia variegata 'Candida'

English: *Parkinsonia, Jerusalem Thorn, Mexican Palo Verde, Palo Verde*

Spanish: *Palo Verde, Lluvia de Oro, Retama, Cina-Cina (Paraguay)*

PARKINSONIA

Family: *Fabaceae*

Parkinsonia aculeata

Native from southern USA to northern South America and the West Indies, there are several Parkinsonia species and even a few hybrids. A hardy, short lived tree (15-25 years), it's green bark gives it the vernacular—Palo Verde, in times of extended drought it will perform photosynthesis through it's green limbs.

Due to it's thorns, this is definitely a tree for a specific kind of site, and you want to put it where it can be seen, because when the Jerusalem Thorn blooms it produces masses of wonderful bright yellow flowers.

Plant in full sun, little to moderate water, will reach 30ft. (9m), drought-tolerant, suitable for xeriscaping, fast growing, blooms late spring through early summer, flowers are fragrant, attractive to bees, propagate from seed. Seed collecting: allow seedheads to dry on plants then remove and collect seeds.

This plant may be considered a protected species in some areas so it is advisable to check before digging or gathering seeds.

However, in Australia this plant has been declared a weed of national significance.

Danger: Plant has a straight spine at the base of each leaf, use extreme caution when handling.

PINK POUI or CUBAN TABEBUIA

Family: *Bignoniaceae*

Tabebuia heterophylla

English: *Pink Poui, Pink Trumpet Tree, Pink Cedar, White Cedar, Pink Tabebuia, Pink Tecoma*

Spanish: *Roble Blanco, Roble de Yugo, Amapola, Amapa Rosa, Matilisquate, Palo Blanco, Roble de Savana*

National flower of El Salvador.

This beautiful deciduous with its clusters of pink trumpet flowers is a native from Mexico to Venezuela. An outstanding yard tree, it also makes an excellent shade tree for coffee and cacao trees. Reliable, strong against the elements, pest free, the wood is used for interior finishing in homes.

Plant in full sun and well drained soil, average water, will reach over 40ft. (12m), blooms late winter through early summer, blooms range from near white through pinks, rose and mauve. Propagate from cuttings, air layering and seed—sow indoors before last frost, outdoors direct sow after last frost. Seed collecting, allow pods to dry on plant then break open to collect seeds. Fast grower, will flower when only two years old.

Also known as the Cuban Pink Trumpet Tree or Cuban Tabebuia; *Tabebuia pallida* is considered a synonym of *Tabebuia heterophylla*. USDA.

CUBAN TABEBUIA
Tabebuia pallida

CUBAN TABEBUIA FLOWER
Tabebuia pallida

RED POWDER PUFF TREE

Family: *Fabaceae*

Calliandra haematocephala

English: *Powder Puff Tree, Redhead Calliandra, Blood Red Tassel Flower*

Spanish: *Calliandra, Granolino*

Fast growers, this family of trees is native in the sub tropical band from India to Madagascar, South America, Mexico, and the United States, has at least 100 species and varieties including shrub and dwarf. Called Lehua's in Hawaii, native species reach 100ft. (30m), and are sacred to the volcano goddess Pele.

The specie's name derives from the Greek, *Calliandra* for "beautiful stamens" and *haematocephala* for "with blood-red head"!

Plant in sun to partial shade, average water needs, likes moist well drained soil, will reach at least 15ft. (4.7m), bloom spring through summer, attractive to hummingbirds, bees and butterflies, propagate from cuttings or from seed. Germinate in a damp paper towel. After some added water during establishment, no further care is needed. Fertilize for best performance Some species make good container plants, some are used in bonsai.

Flattened seed pods open explosively from the tip to the base, ejecting the seeds several yards (metres) away.

WHITE POWDER PUFF TREE
Calliandra haematocephala 'alba'

QUEEN OF FLOWERS

Family: *Lythraceae*

Lagerstroemia speciosa

English: *Queen of Flowers, Pride of India, Queen Crepe Myrtle, Queen Flower, Queen Lager, June Rose*

Spanish: *Reina de las Flores, Astromelia,*

Speciosa comes from the Latin meaning pleasing to the eye, and this beautiful deciduous tree with a brilliant floral display of very showy pink to purple flowers is a royal treat during the summer. A native of India where it's known locally as "jarool", it is prized for it's tough, hardy, reddish wood used in home building, furniture, boats, docks and wharves.

Inconspicuous oval brown fruit, about 0.5inch (1.2cm), splits in six pieces when mature. The seeds are small with winged flaps. There has been much research done on speciosa leaves and their ability to reduce blood sugar, and its insulin-like attributes. Used to treat diabetes and liver ailments, in weight loss products, a natural insulin and glucose transport activator.

Plant in full sun, fast grower up to 40-60ft. (12-18m), 20ft. (6m) is more common, moderate water, drought resistant, low salt tolerance, tolerates alkaline soil, needs good drainage, blooms late spring into mid summer, propagate from cuttings, root suckers, and seed. Attractive peeling bark, easily damaged, the leaves turn red before falling in autumn. Valued for it's tough red timber, medicinal use and ornamental beauty.

English: *Rattlebox Tree, Scarlet Wisteria, False Poinciana, Red Sesbania, Chinese Rattlebox*
Spanish: *Arbol de Traqueteo, Sesbania*

RATTLEBOX TREE

Family: *Fabaceae*

Sesbania punicea

These small deciduous tree/ shrubs from South America, (Argentina, Brazil, Paraguay, and Uruguay), are both very popular and considered an invasive. The plant matures in one year and can produce thousands of seeds per year in winged seedpods. Each pod contains 3-9 seeds, which create a distinct rattling sound when shaken. The pods may stay on the plant through the winter and eventually break open, releasing thousands of seeds The seeds have a very high germination rate and can form dense thickets as they grow. Vibrant and very attractive red-orange flowers in hanging clusters appear in late spring.

Plant in full sun, fast grower, will reach 12-15ft. (3.6-4.7m), very high moisture needs, suitable for bogs and water gardens, blooms repeatedly starting in mid-spring, propagate from seed, direct sow outdoors in autumn. Seed collecting is not recommended for this plant, may not come true from seed. Can be trained into a small-trunk tree. May be considered a noxious weed or invasive in some areas.

Danger: All parts of the plant, particularly the seeds, are poisonous and highly toxic. If ingested, they can be fatal to mammals, birds and reptiles.

RED SILK COTTON

Family: *Bombacaceae*

Bombax ceiba

English: *Red Silk Cotton Tree, Shaving Brush Tree, Kapok Tree, Silk Cotton Tree*

Spanish: *Bombax, Lana, Palo de Lana*

National tree of Guatemala. Sacred to the Maya.

Native to India and dry areas of Asia and Australia and even Central America, the Red Silk Cotton tree is part of the 150+ species of Shaving Brush Trees in the Bombax family. The tree is grown for its easy to work wood, and seeds, on large plantations in India. The seeds contain a large quantity of low-quality kapok, 9-13lbs (4-6kg) per tree, to be used for life belts, cushions, refrigeration insulation, sound proofing, pillows and mattresses. The flowers, seed oil and gum resin all have commercial purposes.

Plant in full sun, likes dry soil with good moisture supply, will reach 50-75ft. (15-23m), but has been reported at 140ft. (43m), fast grower, spectacular red blooms in mid spring, propagate from seed and cuttings. Seed collection and storage: ripe fruits are collected before they open, dried in the sun to open and release the seeds and cotton. The seeds are separated from the floss by putting them in gunny sacks and thrashing with a stick. Grown for ornamental flowers, huge dimensions, and for commercial value. Attractive to bees and hummingbirds.

ROYAL POINCIANA

Family: *Fabaceae*

Delonix regia

English: *Poinciana, Flamboyant, Royal Poinciana, Flame Tree*

Spanish: *Framboyán, Framboyán Rojo, Flamboyán, Arbol de Fuego*

Consistently voted among the top five most beautiful flowering trees in the world, the Royal Poinciana is native to Madagascar and related to the Tamarind and Mimosa trees. The astonishing red flowers bloom in dense clusters which create a solid picture of colour. The older the tree, the more intensely it will bloom.

Deciduous, in winter the tree allows sun to penetrate while in hot months its fine loose leaves provide a wonderful dappled shade beneath.

Plant in full sun, fast growing, great shade tree, will reach 40ft. (15m), drought-tolerant, suitable for xeriscaping, blooms late spring early summer for 4-8 weeks. Propagate from seed, start outdoors mid-winter, in covered containers, coldframe or unheated greenhouse—scarify seed before sowing. Seed collecting, allow pods to dry on plant then break open to collect seeds, properly cleaned, seed can be successfully stored.

SAUSAGE TREE

Family: *Bignoniaceae*

Kigelia africana

English: *Sausage Tree, African Sausage Tree*

Spanish: *Arbol de la Salchicha, Aplo de Salchichón*

Zulu: *Amabelendlovu*

From the African savanna, where many animals take advantage of the dense shade, large flowers (for nectar) and fruits, the night blooming Sausage Tree is a lofty wide-spreading tree often cultivated as an ornamental for its cylindrical fruits, which weigh up to 15lbs (6kg) each. The fruits, very similar to large sausages, are eaten by baboons in the wild.

The wine coloured blooms dangle down in long candelabras, bloom at night, wither and fall at dawn. Some say the fragrance is a dramatic rotting meat strength!

Plant in full sun, will reach over 40ft. (12m), blooms late winter through early spring, fragrant flowers are attractive to night fliers like bats. Propagate from seed; germinate in vitro gelatin, direct sow outdoors in autumn. Seed collecting, allow pods to dry on plant, break open to collect seeds.

Danger: Seed is poisonous if ingested.

English: *Shaving Brush Tree, Bombax, Wool & Cotton Tree*

Spanish: *Arbol de Hisopo, Lana, Palo de Lana, Bombax*

SHAVING BRUSH TREE

Family: *Bombacaceae*

Pseudobombax ellipticum

From the Greek bombyx for silk, this native of Central America has some of the most attention getting flowers on any plant. Flower petals are fused together in a cigar shape and burst open at night revealing the fabulous flower at first light. The flowers are a thick brush of pink stamens, hence the name Shaving Brush Tree. They come in winter before the leaves, new leaves are burgundy then turn green for the summer.

A fast grower, plant in full sun to light shade, average water - less in the winter, will reach 50ft.+ (15m), drought-tolerant, suitable for xeriscaping, will make a great potted plant if kept trimmed. Propagate from woody stem or hardwood cuttings or from seed. Germinate seed in vitro in gelatin, agar or other medium. At least 150 species of trees in the Bombax family.

SHAVING BRUSH TREE FLOWER
Pseudobombax ellipticum

English: *Silk Floss Tree, Floss Silk Tree, Kapok Tree*

Spanish: *Ceiba del Brasil*

SILK FLOSS TREE

Family: *Bombacaceae*

Chorisia speciosa

This magnificent deciduous tropical from Brasil and Argentina is considered by many to be among the most beautiful trees in the world. Known for it's amazing flower display and radical spikes protecting it's trunk and limbs, Silk Floss trees bloom

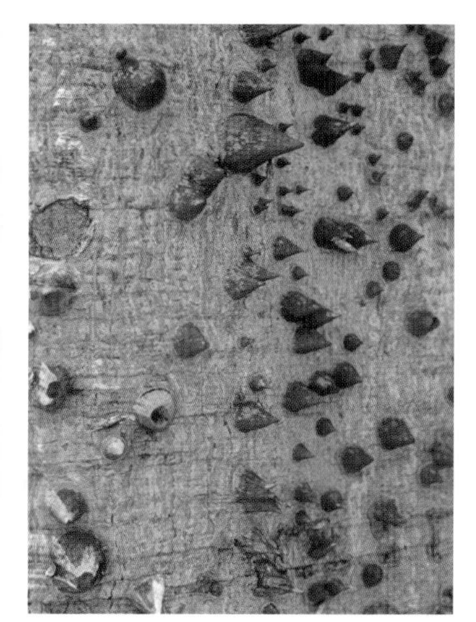

with abandon each autumn producing profuse amounts of large pink, rose, purple, or burgundy flowers. The flowers are followed by pear shaped inedible fruits filled with many seeds embedded in silky white floss. When mature they split, releasing the seed and floss.

Chorisia taxonomy is not fully refined with many variations in the flowers (see pictures) so there is a good chance that several different species and hybrids are lumped under the name *C. speciosa*. Many botanists feel that the flowers of Pseudobombax ellipticumno two trees are exactly alike.

Plant in full sun and well drained soil, average water, does not compete well with lawn grasses, will reach 60ft. (18m), autumn bloomer, propagate from seed, fairly fast grower, hardy, no pests, excellent choice in any landscape. Seed collecting, allow to dry then break open to collect. Trunk becomes bottle shaped as it ages, the seedpod silk has been used to stuff cushions.

Danger: Plant has spikes on trunk and limbs use caution when handling.

SILK FLOSS TREE FLOWER
Chorisia speciosa

English: *Spicy Jatropha, Peregrina*
Spanish: *Peregrina de Rojo*

SPICY JATROPHA

Family: *Euphorbiaceae*

Jatropha integerrima

This wonderful Cuba native is grown mainly for its spectacular year-round flower display. Jatrophas can be trained to be bushy, or climb up trellises depending on your needs. They make a wonderful small, or patio, tree. Blooms range from red-orange to coral, apricot and scarlet. Very popular with owners and gardeners.

Plant in light shade, can take some full sun, will reach 8-10ft. (2.4-3m), regular water, blooms repeatedly all year, profusely in summer, seldom need fertilizer, drought-tolerant, suitable for xeriscaping, propagate from cuttings—let dry for a day before planting, or from seed, direct sow outdoors in autumn. Seed collecting, allow seedheads to dry on plants then remove and collect seeds. Low maintenance. Popular.

Danger: All parts of this plant are poisonous if ingested and like all of the Euphorbia family, the sap can be irritating to bare skin.

TRAVELER'S PALM

Family: *Musaceae*

Ravenala madagascariensis

English: *Traveler's Palm, Traveler's Tree*
Spanish: *Arbol del Viajero, Palma del Viajero*

A Madagascar native, Traveler's Palm is not a true palm, but a tree and is related to banana plants and bird-of-paradise varieties. Well maintained the leaves produce a beautiful half moon fan with clusters of flowers in the same shape as the Bird-Of-Paradise flowers, only larger.

The name derives from the flower bracts and large hollow leafed stalks which can hold up to a quart (litre) of water, so a thirsty traveler may always find emergency refreshment.

Plant in full sun, can reach over 40ft. (12m), average water, requires rich, moist, well drained soil, bloom colour white & green, attractive to bees, butterflies and birds, propagate by seeds in spring or division of suckers anytime, self-sows freely, dead-head if you do not want volunteer seedlings. Can also be grown indoors or in the greenhouse.

English: *Tree Hibiscus, Mountain Mahoe, Cuban Bast, Blue Mahoe*

Spanish: *Majagua, Majagua Azul, Emajagua Excelsa*

National tree of Jamaica.

TREE HIBISCUS

Family: *Malvaceae*

Hibiscus elatus

Native to Jamaica and upland parts of Cuba, but widely planted and naturalized from south Florida to Brazil, and throughout the West Indies. The name Mahoe is derived from a Caribe Indian word and the "blue" refers to blue-green streaks in the polished wood, giving it that distinctive appearance. The flowers, which last a single day, are large and funnel shaped, changing colour during the day from yellow to bronze and then red before dropping at nightfall.

The Blue Mahoe is so beautiful and durable that it is prized for cabinet work, fine furniture, inlay work, picture frames, bowls, art carvings and interior trim. The wood has a musical quality and has been used in the making of cuatros: the classic Caribbean Latin "guitar" developed in Puerto Rico from the 17th century onward. The inner bark of the tree is often referred to as Cuba bark because it was used for tying bundles of Havana cigars.

Plant in full sun to partial shade, average water to start, well drained soil, rapid grower to average height of 80ft. (24m), often used in reforestation, resistant to decay fungi, propagate by seed or cuttings.

VERA WOOD

Family: *Zygophyllaceae*

Bulnesia arborea

English: *Vera Wood, Maracaibo Lignum Vitae*
Spanish: *Guayacán o Palo Santo*

Vera Wood is an evergreen tree native to Columbia and Venezuela and is cultivated for its buttery-yellow flowers and valuable hard and heavy timber called Vera Wood or Maracaibo Lignum Vitae. Introduced from Venezuela to South Florida by Dr. David Fairchild (Fairchild Tropical Gardens), they produce bright yellow flowers in pairs at each branch tip, while fruits are winged pods produced bi-annually.

Plant in full sun, slow to medium grower, will reach as much as 100ft. (30m), but 30-40ft. (9-12m) is more common. Moderate water, drought resistant, additional watering not needed once established, needs good drainage, tolerates poor soils, fertilize twice a year. Blooms spring through autumn. Propagate from seed, which germinate in about a month, or air layering. Great shade tree.

English: *White Bird of Paradise, Giant Bird of Paradise, Natal Wild Banana*

Spanish: *Pajáro Blanco, Strelitzia, Ave Blanco de Paraiso*

Zulu: *Isagudu, Isigude*

WHITE BIRD OF PARADISE

Family: *Strelitziaceae*

Strelitzia nicolai

This wonderful native of South Africa is related to traveler's palms and the bananas. It grows with multiple trunks in a clumping style always expanding its diameter. The species name 'nicolai' was selected to honour the Russian Tsar Nicolas II.

It flowers in clusters on the stem, large bluish flower buds are produced in early spring, these slowly open to release the huge tropical white flowers enclosed within. The flowers' stamen are blue in colour with white pollen, after several days this pollen slowly turns yellow.

The White Bird must be given consideration in landscaping because of its dense stems and expansionist tendencies. Plant away from the home, the torn leaf appearance and the flowers look better viewed from a distance.

Plant in full sun to partial shade, will reach up to 30ft. (9m), blooms from early spring through summer, easy grow, low maintenance, regular water in well draining soil, propagate by dividing clumps in spring or from seed. Research further propagation methods. Attractive to bees, butterflies and birds, makes a good container and indoor plant. Very attractive for landscaping!

Danger: Parts of the plant are poisonous if ingested.

YELLOW POINCIANA

Family: *Fabaceae*

Peltophorum pterocarpum

English: *Yellow Poinciana, Yellow Flame Tree, Copper-Pod Tree, Yellow Flamboyant Tree*

Spanish: *Framboyán Amarillo*

Multiple Latin synonyms and common names.

Native to coastal areas from Sri Lanka through the Malay archipelago and Indonesia to northern Australia, as well as south America—depending on species; Yellow Poinciana is an upright, fast growing, very showy flowering tree. Part of the 200 genera in the Fabaceae family, there are three species in Peltophorum.

Planted as specimen or shade trees they are very popular as street trees in tropical cities, and commonly planted for shade in tropical and subtropical gardens.

Plant in light shade to full sun, vigorous fast grower to 50ft. (15m) tall with nice umbrella spread, moderate water, prefers moist, well-drained soil, somewhat drought resistant, fantastic displays of fragrant bright yellow flowers, blooms late spring through summer, cannot tolerate frost, dark green leathery leaflets, elongated seedpods, propagate from seed—that must be treated before they will germinate. Easy to grow, wonderful fragrance, maintenance free winner!

YLANG YLANG

Family: *Annonaceae*

Cananga odorata

English: *Ylang Ylang, Perfume Tree, Channel Tree, Ilang Ilang*

Spanish: *Ilan-Ilan, Ilang-Ilang, Cadima, Cananga*

Made famous by Coco Chanel who in 1923 said upon introducing Chanel No.5 in Paris, *"I wanted a perfume that is composed—not hints of roses or lilies of the valley. A woman's perfume—redolent, evocative of a woman. A perfume unlike any other ever made. The ideal scent for a woman."*

The Chanel No.5 Perfume Tree is native to Southern India, Java, Malaysia, the Philippines and other Pacific islands. It's common name is Ylang-Ylang, pronounced (ee-lang ee-lang) and is among the most celebrated flowering trees in the world. It is cultivated for its unusual and wonderfully scented blooms whose distilled oil is used in Chanel No.5.

The tree is part of a Philippine fairytale; fertilized by moths at night, ylang ylang oil extract of various qualities is used in soap, detergent, perfume, an aromatherapy cure all, cosmetics, and body oil.

Plant in full sun to partial shade, regular water, easy care, low maintenance, will reach 60ft. (18m), very fragrant, blooms constantly, propagate from seed, sow indoors before last frost. Can be grown in tubs in cooler climates, but must be kept warm. Research seed collecting and sowing.

BANANA FRONDS - BAY ISLANDS, HONDURAS

Chapter 12

Tropical Fruit Trees

Tropical fruit trees have been witness to momentous moments in history, embroiled in politics, intrigue and war. Made and broken careers, fortunes and lives. Used as everything from money to medicine, housing and of course food.

Coffee, among other things, made Lloyds the insurance giant it is today. Cocoa pods and seeds were used as money by the ancient Maya. Chicle is used in the manufacturing of chewing gum, while breadfruit gave Captain Bligh his nickname—old breadfruit Bligh - and was one of numerous fruit trees he brought to the New World. Bananas and breadfruit feed the tropical and developing world to this day.

While many tropical fruits are a gift from the New World to the Old, nearly all citrus fruits come from the Old World and reached the New World via the Spanish, in fact the first lemon seeds came across the Atlantic to Hispaniola with Christopher Columbus in 1493. The grapefruit is thought to be of Caribbean origin and is actually the state of Florida's most valuable fruit export, while oranges have become the most commonly grown citrus tree in the world.

Citrus trees and their fruit are easily recognizable by most everyone from childhood, and as such have not been included in the book.

For the home gardener citrus trees can be more difficult to grow successfully than one might realize. They are subject to a great number of diseases, viruses, canker and blight that can affect every part of the tree. Before deciding to grow citrus trees it is highly recommended that one read up on everything from planting to pests, diseases, pruning and maintenance, not to mention local laws and politics.

English: *Ackee, Akee, Akee Apple Tree, Achee, Vegetable Brains*

Spanish: *Akee, Seso Vegetal, Arbol de Seso, Palo de Seso (Cuba)*

ACKEE

Family: *Sapindaceae*

Blighia sapida

Indigenous to the forests of the Ivory and Gold Coast's of Africa, its name is derived from the West African Akye Fufo. The scientific name, *Blighia Sapida*, is in honour of the infamous Captain William Bligh, who brought the fruit from West Africa to Kew in Jamaica in 1793.

The fruit turns bright red on reaching maturity and splits open along the seams with continued exposure to the sun—yawning. When open it reveals three large black shiny seeds and bright yellow flesh. Traditionally it is at this time that the ackees are harvested.

ATTENTION! It is only the fleshy arils around the seeds that are edible. When boiled, drained and simmered in oil with salted dried cod, your choice of vegetables and hot peppers, it becomes Jamaica's national dish, Ackee and Saltfish.

ACKEE FRUIT ▲

▼ OPEN ACKEE FRUIT

Canned arils are exported to the United Kingdom where they are welcomed by Jamaican immigrants, but importation into the US has been banned by the United States Food and Drug Administration.

Plant in sun to partial shade, average water, will reach to 40ft. (12m), easy maintenance free, fast growing tree. Propagate from seeds or by shield-budding. In European greenhouses, cuttings of ripe shoots are rooted in sand and raised in a mixture of peat and loam.

Danger: Contains hypoglycin A and B. The fruit and seeds of this tree are always poisonous, and even the seed coating if not eaten at the right time is poisonous. Never force open an ackee pod, allow to open naturally.

Ackee poisoning in humans is evidenced by acute vomiting, sometimes repeated, followed by drowsiness, convulsions, coma and, too often, death.

ALMOND TREE

Family: *Combretaceae*

Terminalia catappa

English: *Almond Tree, Tropical Almond, Indian Almond, Malabar Almond*

Spanish: *Almendra, Almendro de la India, Alcornoque, Almendrón, Almendro*

Originally from the Malay Peninsula, Almond thrives as an ornamental, shade and large landscape tree in tropical cities all over the world.

The tree has a characteristic pagoda shape and leaves form a rosette found only at the end of a branch. During the dry season, the leaves turn into autumn colours of red, copper, and gold. The tree usually sheds all its leaves twice a year. The green almond-shaped fruit turns red to purple when ripe, can be eaten raw with oil extracted from the dried nuts used in cooking.

ALMOND FRUIT

Used by many cultures in a large variety of traditional medicine tropical almond is also used by breeders of tropical aquarium fish to keep them healthy.

Plant in full sun, well drained soil, average water, will reach average height of 30-40ft. (9-12m), reported to 90ft. (27m), flowers are inconspicuous, salt and drought tolerant, can be grown in container for early years, propagate by seed, host tree for fruit flies. Considered an invasive in many parts of the world. Fast grower. Fruits will stain clothes and pavements. Birds and bats love the ripe fruit.

AVOCADO TREE

Family: *Lauraceae*

Persea americana

English: *Avocado, Alligator Pear, Avocado Pear*
Spanish: *Aguacate, Palta, Cura, Cupandra*

One of the world's most famous and trendy fruits, the avocado originated in southern Mexico and was being cultivated throughout the Americas before the arrival of Europeans.

High in monosaturates, the oil content of avocados is second only to olives, and has been shown that avocado oil can reduce blood cholesterol levels in humans.

There are three main types, West Indian, Guatemala and Mexican, with a multitude of hybrids and cultivars. Each panicle of flowers will produce only one to three fruits in a complex pollination process. Some cultivars bloom and set fruit in alternate years. Commercial standards requires fruit to reach 8% oil content before harvesting.

Plant in sun to partial shade, average water, do not overwater, will reach heights over 40ft. (12m), blooms mid-spring into early summer, attractive to bees and hoverflies. Dwarf cultivars are suitable pot and indoor plants. Propagate by grafting or air layering. Every kid has stuck three toothpicks in an avo pip and hung it in a jar of water to watch the roots begin. Grafted plants normally produce fruit within one to two years, seeds 8-20 years. The roots are highly competitive and will choke out nearby plants, plus raise pavement., while shade under the trees is too dense to garden under.

Danger: Parts of the plant, leaves & bark are poisonous if ingested; unripe fruit can be toxic.

English: *Banana, Banana Tree, Banana Shrub*
Spanish: *Banana, Plátano, Guineos, Bananero, Banano*

BANANAS

Family: *Musaceae*

Genus: *Musa*

One of the ancient wonder plants with over 70 species and over 300 edible forms, bananas and plantains have played a significant role in human civilization and constitute a crucial part of human diets in all tropical regions.

Originally from the Malay Peninsula, the word 'banana' comes from coastal West Africa, and was adopted in the New World for the sweet forms with yellow skin. The word 'plantain' comes from the Spanish and refers to the starchy cooking bananas, which often have green or red skins. The sweet banana is very easily digested, but the plantain must be boiled, steamed, roasted, or deep fried before eating.

Today there are huge commercial operations exporting bananas from tropical regions, however the majority of bananas, 85%, are grown by small farmers in tropical countries for local consumption. Musa has a wide variety of uses including cattle feed, clothing, medicine, dye, roofs, alcohol, wine, vinegar, and packing material.

In the same plot of land where one could harvest 98lbs (44kg) of white potatoes or 33lbs (15kg) of wheat, a person could also harvest 4400lbs (2,000kg) of bananas with very little labour. Bananas are very rich in carbohydrates, vitamin C, A, & B, minerals potassium, copper, magnesium, calcium, and iron. Annual world production of Musa fruit exceeds 40 million metric tons.

BANANA FLOWER

ORNATE BANANA
Musa omata

ORNATE BANANA FLOWER
Musa omata

Bananas from ornamental and dwarf, to exotic ones with names like, Thousand Fingers, Rajapuri, African Rhino and Burmese Blue, are available today.

Easy to grow, research for variety, growing, fruit, flowers, pruning & propagation before purchasing and planting. Related to Heliconias and travelers palms, not actually a tree but a herbaceous perennial, with the fruit technically a berry. Good indoor and hothouse plants. Plant in full sun to partial shade, provide wind protection for whole leaf look, lots of water and rich soil. From planting to your first bananas takes about 18 months. After fruiting the plant dies but has already produced new pups to continue the cycle. A bunch of bananas is called a 'hand' and ripening on commercial plantations is often hastened by covering the hand with a plastic bag.

RED TORCH BANANA FLOWER
Musa coccinea

BANANA COMMERCIAL

RED TORCH BANANA
Musa coccinea

GOLDEN LOTUS
Musella lasiocarpa

GOLDEN LOTUS FLOWER
Musella lasiocarpa

BREADFRUIT TREES

Family: *Moraceae*

Artocarpus altilis

English: *Breadfruit, Breadfruit Tree*

Spanish: *Arbol de Pan, Palo de Pan, Fruita de Pan, Mazapán, Panapén*

The legendary tree of *The Mutiny On The Bounty*, the Breadfruit (seedless varieties) and Breadnut (edible seeded varieties) are probably native to the Malay archipelago. The French actually brought it to the West Indies 20 years before Bligh and in fact the Spanish probably brought it over from the Philippines many years before that. Breadfruit has been cultivated since prehistoric times and is a massive multi-use tree and fruit. There are over 400 varieties and cultivars.

Key to Polynesian expansion throughout the south seas, the wood made light canoe hulls, drums and household articles, all parts of the tree have a milky, gummy latex sap which was used to caulk seams and as a sticky lime to snare birds. It's bark was used as a source of fiber for tapa.

The breadfruit can be consumed as a fruit when ripe or as a vegetable when underripe. Today it continues in all uses including flour for pastries and breads, domestic animal feed, and in an endless variety of preparation, boiled, baked, steamed, roasted, pureed, fried, you name it, for human consumption.

A close relative is the JACK FRUIT TREE (*Artocarpus heterophyllus*) with large oblong fruits that weigh up to 70lbs (32kg) each.

Plant in full sun, rich moist soil, high humidity, lots of rainfall or water, will reach 30ft. (9m), has been recorded to 85ft. (26m). Fast growing. Very sensitive to cold weather. Propagate from seed or stem cuttings, seeds have limited shelf life.

Danger: Most varieties of breadfruit are purgative if eaten raw. Some varieties are boiled twice and the water thrown away to avoid unpleasant effects, while there are a few named cultivars that can be safely eaten without cooking.

BREADNUT TREES
Artocarpus altilis

English: *Breadnut Tree, Jak Fruit, Jackfruit Tree*

Spanish: *Pana de Pepitas, Castaña, Castaño del Malabar, Chataigne, Arbol del Pan, Fruta del Pobre, Jaca, Jaqueiro*

BREADNUT TREE ▲
Artocarpus altilis ▼

JACK FRUIT TREE - FRUIT
Artocarpus heterophyllus

COCOA TREE

Family: *Sterculiaceae*

Theobroma cacao

English: *Cocoa Tree, Cacao, Chocolate Tree*

Spanish: *Cacáo, Caceteiro, Caca-uatl, Truijillanc*

The extraordinary Chocolate Tree.

Perfectly named by Swedish botanist Karl von Linne; Theobroma—meaning "food of the gods". The ancient Maya first cultivated the Chocolate Tree about 1,500 years ago, concocting chocolate drinks 'chocolatl' (pronounced: cho-kil-what-til), while the precious beans were used as currency. Delightfully addictive the church saw it as an evil drug banning it's use to no avail.

A South American native now cultivated pantropically, selected pods are roasted, then the kernels are pressed through rollers and the result is a dark brown paste called chocolate liquor. Chocolate liquor is the base product from which all chocolate is made, with worldwide production of chocolate now at more than a million tons annually.

Cacao seeds are also the source of commercial cocoa, cocoa butter, soaps, cosmetics, emollients, herbal & traditional medicines, and of course Coca-Cola!

Research indicates that a tiny fly is the primary (if not only) pollinator of the complex cacao flowers, and without its work, there would be no chocolate.

Plant in light shade, will reach varying height from 15-30ft. (5-9m), bears flowers and fruit all year, average water, propagate by cuttings, buddings or graftings, but seeding is cheaper. Seeds germinate at maturity, and are viable only a short time, plant in shaded pots, transplant when 24inches (60cm) into shaded area. Pods can be green, yellow/golden, red to purple in colour.

COCOA FRUIT

COCOA FLOWER

CHICLE TREE

Family: *Sapotaceae*

Manilkara zapota

English: *Chicle, Chewing Gum Tree, Sapodilla, Naseberry, Noseberry*

Spanish: *Níspero, Zapote, Chicozapote, Zapotillo, Muyozapot*

Native to the tropical forests of the Yucatán Peninsula, Belize, and northern Guatemala, the ancient Maya, who cultivated and tapped the Chicle tree, used to call this Zapotle. In fact Mayan writings talk about 'millions' of Zapotle trees at the peak of their civilization, and even today, Sapodilla is the most abundant tree in the jungles of the Gran Petén.

Chicle is the milky juice or latex of the Sapodilla tree and the source of chicle for chewing gum, and of the word —Chiclets! The Maya were exploited as chicleros to work plantations until the start of the Second World War and the subsequent scarcity of resources ended the practice. Collected during the rainy season gum is obtained by tapping the trees every 2-3 years. Although natural Chicle is still used, most of today's chewing gums are made from a synthetic vinyl gum base.

Plant in full sun, average water, well drained soil, will reach 60ft. (18m), inconspicuous blooms, large 3inch (8cm) fruit, drought tolerant, propagate from seed, protect from frost. The sweet fruit is a favorite in the tropics, can be eaten raw, or made into syrups and preserves.

CHICLE FRUIT

CHICLE FLOWER

COCONUT PALM

Family: *Arecaceae*

Cocos nucifera

English: *Coconut Palm, Coco Palm*

Spanish: *Coco, Palma de Coco, Cocotero, Palmera*

'The' signature tree of the tropics, the coconut palm is the most recognized tree in the world. It simply says tropical.

Scholars feel the coconut palm originated in the south Pacific, however there is evidence that ancestral coconut palms may have originated in western Gondwana, when the continent split from Pangea around the end of the Paleozoic. It self seeded around the world's tropical zone as coconuts float, wash up on beaches and germinate.

A significant cash crop and economically important, throughout the tropics oil, fibre, fruit, food, thatch, mats, clothing and construction materials all derive from the coconut palm.

There are many varieties and variations with the old Jamaica Tall being the most recognized. Malayan varieties are most resistant to Lethal Yellowing disease, the scourge of coconut palms. There are also dwarf, tall and cultivar varieties, with the huge rare, Seychelle native, Double Coconut whose nuts may weigh as much as 40-45 pounds (18-20kg) each, and are the largest seeds on the planet.

Plant in full sun, will reach heights of over 40ft. (12m) - depending on species. Bloom repeatedly, require consistently moist soil, propagate from seed. Research before choosing species for your garden.

Danger: Most palms require fronds and nuts to be trimmed before hurricane season—a coconut traveling at 125mph (200kph) has the destructive capability of a cannonball.

FLOWER SPRAY

GREEN MALAYAN

COFFEE TREE

Family: *Rubiaceae*

Coffea arabica

English: *Coffee Tree, Arabicar*
Spanish: *Café, Cafeto*

The history and development of the beverage coffee is a wonderful story. Originally from Ethiopia, Arab traders began early cultivation 1,000 years ago. Through guile, wit, intrigue, love affairs, trade and wars, the bean slowly spread across the globe, making coffee barons in Brazil, insurance giant Lloyds, the governor of Mecca to be executed and Pope Clement VIII to baptize it as an acceptable Christian beverage.

The Dutch managed to smuggle out the first beans and become the first to transport and cultivate coffee commercially, in Sri Lanka and in their East Indian colony, Java —source of the brew's nickname.

Decaf, instant, freeze dried, vacuum packed, cappuccino and expresso all have fascinating stories to tell.

Arabica is the most widely grown species for producing coffee. A small tree in the wild, it is often cultivated as a shrub

and pruned to a height of 6ft. (1.8m) for easier harvesting. Mountain grown, shade covered, and sun dried is now de rigueur in coffee circles.

Plant in light shade, average water, will reach 12-15ft. (3.6-4.5m), tiny white blooms in mid-spring, propagate from seed, suitable for growing indoors. Seed collecting, remove fleshy coating on seeds before storing.

COFFEE BERRIES

GUYANA CHESTNUT

Family: *Malvaceae*

Pachira aquatica

English: *Guyana (Guiana) Chestnut, Money Tree, Malabar Chestnut, Provision Tree, French Peanut, Wild Cocoa Tree, Fortune Tree, Water Chestnut*

Spanish: *Maní Francés, Árbol de Dinero, Árbol de la Suerte, Castaño*

This amazing native from tropical Mexico to northern Brazil is a fast growing fruit tree that produces huge pods containing edible seed kernels or nuts which dry on the plant, then split and expel the kernels. High in fat and protein, the seeds can be eaten raw or cooked while the leaves and flowers are eaten as vegetables, and the bark is used in traditional medicine.

Frequently sold for good luck and potted like small bonsai trees with braided trunks.

Has highly evolved leaves and chlorophyll-containing green branches.

Plant in full sun to partial shade, regular water, likes wet environments, will reach 75ft.+ (23m+) in the wild, 30ft. (9m) in landscaping, does not take frost or freezes, blooms spring through autumn, each fragrant bloom lasts a single day, attractive to bats, low maintenance, easy to grow, nutritious fruit, suitable for growing in pots and indoors, propagate from seed, cuttings and air layering.

Very similar species to MALABAR CHESTNUT (*Bombax glabrum*): they share common names and even the scientific identities are often switched. The Malabar Chestnut has all white fragrant flowers and smallish elongated fruit pods, while the Guyana Chestnut flowers have red stamens with large fruit pods covered in a brown tomentum.

English: *Litchi Tree, Chinese Cherry, Leechee, Lichee, Litchi, Lychee*

Spanish: *Lechia*

LITCHI TREE

Family: *Sapindaceae*

Litchi chinensis

Native to southern China, the Litchi has been in recorded history for the past one thousand years. Related to the Golden Rain Tree and the Ackee fruit tree, the Litchi is a slow grower and seedling trees will not bear fruit until they are 5 to 25 years old, reach prime at 30-40 years and will bear fruit to 100 years old.

Litchis develop inconspicuous green-white flowers which grow in panicles close to 12inches (30cm) long These panicles then produce very tasty edible 'nuts' borne in large, red clusters of 20-30. They are not actually nuts and the seed is not edible! Under the skin is the fruit which is white translucent, firm, juicy, sweet and delicious. A truly delectable exotic!

Plant in full sun to partial shade, will reach 30-40ft. (9-12m) although very old ones have reached a reported 100ft. (30m). Grow well in all types of soil, high water requirements but must drain well. Blooms mid-spring, propagate from seed, grafting or air layering.

Seed collecting, allow unblemished fruit to ripen, clean and dry seeds. Litchi seeds remain viable only 4 to 5 days and are primarily used as rootstock. Air layering is favoured.

MALABAR CHESTNUT TREE

Family: *Bombacaceae*

Bombax glabrum

English: *French Peanut, Malabar Chestnut, Guiana Chestnut, Provision Tree*

Spanish: *Bombax, Castaño*

Very similar species: Guyana Chestnut (*Pachira aquatica*).

From the island of Madagascar and often confused with the Guyana Chestnut (*Pachira aquatica*); they share common names and even the scientific identities are often switched, the Malabar Chestnut has all white fragrant flowers and smallish elongated fruit pods, while the Guyana Chestnut flowers have red stamens with large fruit pods covered in a brown tomentum.

Plant in full sun to partial shade, average water, will reach to 20ft. (6m), white fragrant flowers, attractive to butterflies and hummingbirds, propagate from seed, cuttings and air layering, suitable for growing indoors and bonsai. Edible seeds with a peanut flavour.

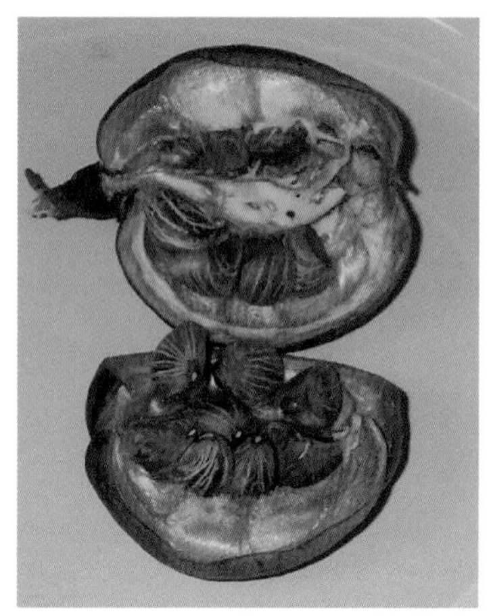

MALAY APPLE TREE

Family: *Myrtaceae*

Syzygium malaccense

English: *Malay Apple, Mountain Apple, Ohia, Otaheite-apple, Pomerac*

Spanish: *Pomarrosa, Manzana, Malaya, Pomagás, Pomagada, Pera*

Another native from Southeast Asia the Malay Apple is sacred to the Polynesians —temple idols are carved from it's wood and the flowers are considered sacred to the volcano goddess Pele—it spread rapidly throughout the Pacific Islands and is featured in Fijian mythology. Yet another tree introduced to the West Indies by Captain Bligh, it is now widely planted throughout the tropics with numerous clones and varieties.

The fruits are made into sauces, preserves, jellies, pickled, wines, and stewed with cloves served with cream as dessert. Flowers are eaten in salads while young leaves and shoots are eaten as greens. Many parts are used in a variety of herbal and traditional medicines.

A delight to the eye in every respect, the Malay apple is much admired for the beauty of the tree, its flowers and its colourful, glistening fruits.

MALAY APPLES

Plant in full sun, fast grower, will reach 60ft. (18m), needs a humid climate with an annual rainfall of 60inches (150cm) or more. Will grow in a wide range of soils, propagate from softwood cuttings, air layering or direct sow outdoors from seed. May flower 2 or 3 times a year, fruits mature in 60 days from the full opening of the flowers, fall soon after ripening and deteriorate rapidly. For marketing, they must be hand-picked to avoid damage and to have longer shelf-life.

English: *Mango*
Spanish: *Mango, Manga*

MANGO TREE

Family: *Anacardiaceae*
Magnifera indica

Originating in India, the Mango has been cultivated for at least 4,000 years, has multiple varieties and variations, and is often referred to as "*king of fruits*". Found throughout the tropics it is one of the most highly consumed fruits in the world.

Mango trees make great shade as well as fruit trees, long-lived with some specimens known to be over 300 years old and still fruiting.

Most of the tiny flowers function as males by providing pollen, but some are bisexual and set fruit. Pollination through flies, wasps, and bees.

Plant in full sun, average water, will reach over 40ft. (12m), blooms in late spring through mid-summer, propagate from seed (stratify if sowing indoors) or by grafting. Seed collecting, allow unblemished fruit to ripen, clean and dry seeds. Seed does not store well, sow as soon as possible. Attractive to bees & butterflies. Dwarf varieties can be container grown.

Danger: Parts of plant are poisonous if ingested.

The mango is in the same botanical family as poison oak/ivy. After eating mango be sure to wash your face and hands carefully. If some mango juice remains on your skin and you are sensitive to it, you will break out in an itchy rash in a few days.

PAPAYA TREE

Family: *Caricaceae*

Carica papaya

English: *Papaya, Pawpaw, Papay, Papaw*

Spanish: *Lechosa, Papaya, Fruta Bomba, Melón Zapote, Papayero, Papayo*

Indigenous to Central America, Papaya, like so many fruits, is another gift from the New World to the Old. The Spanish noticed that the natives were capable of eating large meals without any kind of discomfort from indigestion—reason, they were eating unripe Papaya after every meal. The enzyme papain is found in the Papaya latex, and the most important use of papain is as meat tenderizer.

There are estimates of 20-45 species of Papaya, which is a dioecious tree, so you must have both male and female individuals to produce fruits. The famous cultivar 'Solo' was taken to Hawaii in 1911 and there are now large commercial Papaya plantations on the islands. The fruit's ripe flesh is delicious and sweet.

Plant in full sun to light shade, will reach 20-30ft. (6-9m), blooms repeatedly all year, grown for foliage, fruit and fragrance. Watering is critical, the soil needs to be moist in hot weather and dry in cold weather. A very fast grower, may be considered an invasive, can bear fruit in one year. Rich in Vitamin A, fruit can reach 20lbs (9kg). Propagate from seed, good container and greenhouse plant, attractive to butterflies and moths.

English: *Pomegranate*

Spanish: *Granada, Granado, Mangrano*

POMEGRANATE TREE

Family: *Punicaceae*

Punica granatum

The pomegranate is native from Iran to the Himalayas in northern India and was cultivated and naturalized over the whole Mediterranean region since ancient times. Now cultivated throughout the world, almost all cultures have a common name in their language for the pomegranate. It gave it's name to the first hand grenades as the fruit resembles an old fashioned hand grenade with burning wick—and specially trained grenade throwers were called grenadiers.

Pomegranate fruits are most often consumed as fresh juice or to make jellies, sorbets, hot & cold sauces, as well as to flavour cakes and baked goodies, and even made into a wine. The syrup is sold commercially as grenadine.

Prefer a semi-arid, mild-temperate to subtropical climate, and are naturally adapted to regions with cool winters and hot summers.

Plant in full sun to partial shade, will reach a normal 15-20ft. (4.5-6m), blooms mid-summer, drought tolerant, suitable for xeriscaping, deer resistant, dwarf and cultivars available. Propagate from cuttings (best) or seed. Cuttings root easily and plants from them bear fruit after about 3 years. Seed does not store well, sow as soon as possible.

Danger: Plant has spines use extreme caution when handling.

ROSE APPLE TREE

Family: *Myrtaceae*

Eugenia jambos

English: *Rose Apple, Plum Rose, Jambu, Malabar Plum*

Spanish: *Pomarrosa, Pomo, Mazana Rosa, Jambeiro*

Native of India and Malaya, widely cultivated in the tropics. Thought to be the tree representing the theory of creation that bore the golden fruit of immortality. A prized ornamental and relative of the Malay Apple *Syzygium malaccense*, and Wax Jambu *Syzygium samarangense* fruit trees, flowers and fruits throughout the year.

The globular fruits are up to 2inches (5cm) in length with a thin layer of pale yellow flesh and 1 to 3 brown seeds, which lie loose in a large, hollow seed cavity. The flesh is rose scented, crisp, juicy and sweet. It is sometimes eaten out of hand but is more generally used to make jelly and jams. It can be stewed or preserved in syrup.

Plant in full sun, regular water, will reach 30ft. (9m), propagate by seed, budding or air layering. Seeds remain viable for only a short time after being removed from the fruit. The seeds are unusual in that they are poly embryonic —as many as 7 or 8 plants may arise from a single seed.

Danger: The roots and seeds are considered poisonous.

SEA GRAPE TREE

Family: *Polygonaceae*

Coccoloba uvifera

English: *Sea Grape, Seaside Grape*
Spanish: *Coccoloba*

A Florida and tropical America native, Sea Grape can be a large shrub or tree, depending on nature and pruning. It grows naturally in the wild, along the beaches on coastal dunes and in the tropical hardwood hammocks. Provides food and shelter for wildlife, and is very attractive with lush foliage.

The "grapes" are the seeds and grow in nice clusters, especially where exposed to sun, and a fine jelly can be made when ripe in early summer.

Plant in full sun to partial shade, beach sand is fine, will reach 40ft. (12m), blooms late spring through summer, flowers are tiny, white & fragrant, salt and drought-tolerant, suitable for xeriscaping. Propagate by seed or wood cuttings. Low maintenance.

WAX JAMBU

Family: *Myrtaceae*

Syzygium samarangense

English: *Wax Jambu, Wax Apple, Java Apple, Java Rose Apple, Samarang Rose Apple, Water Apple*

Spanish: *Cajuil de Solimán (DR), Cashu di Surinam, Makopa (Costa Rica), Manzana de Java, Jambeiro*

Multiple Synonyms.

Similar species: Rose Apple (Eugenia jambos).

This native of Malaysia is a popular and beautiful tropical fruit tree whose branches and leaves give it a characteristic pyramid shape. Blooming almost continuously it produces prodigious amounts of fruit – wax jambus are small pinky red fruits that are juicy, crunchy and refreshing especially when chilled.

Plant in full sun, most any soil, average water, fast grower, can reach 40ft. (12m), blooms late spring through autumn, blooms usually pink, also red and white available, lots of edible fruit, bird favorite, propagate by seed, air-layering, grafting or budding. Cannot handle frost or freezes. Grows well throughout the tropics, Florida and California.

WAX JAMBU FRUIT

SCIENTIFIC NAME INDEX

COMMON NAME INDEX

CULTIVARS & VARIETIES - What's the difference?

The words cultivar and variety can be used interchangeably, however with two important distinctions: a cultivar is commercially cultivated for profit, and its name can be registered with plant societies and records.

GLOSSARY & TERMS

Anther: A pollen containing appendage.

Apetalous: Without petals.

Bipinnate: A leaf divided twice in a featherlike pattern.

Bract: Small leaf, or scale below the calyx.

Bulb: Underground stem, sending roots downwards and foliage upwards.

Calyx: Cup like at the base of the flower.

Cerise: Light red colour.

Corolla: Inner portion of the flower surrounding the stamens and protruding from the calyx.

Cultivar: A variety originating from cultivation.

Epiphytic: Air plant, grows without soil.

Filament: The fine hair-like stalk that the anther sits on top of.

Hybrid: Offspring of mixed parentage.

Inflorescence: Arrangement of flowers in relation to the axis and each other.

Lanceolate: Tapered end lance shaped.

Oblong: Rounded at both ends & parallel sides.

Obovate: Similar to the above, but shape is larger towards the end of the leaf.

Ovary: Part of the plant that holds ovules or seeds which grow into fruit.

Ovule: The part of the ovary that becomes the seeds.

Panicle: Loosely arranged flower clusters, sometimes pyramid in shape.

Petal: Individual divisions of the corolla of the flower.

Petiole: The leaf stalk.

Pinnate: The leaflets are symmetrically divided along the leaf axis.

Pistil: The female organ of the flower, consists of ovary, style, and stigma.

Pseudobulbs: Formed from parts other than the ovary.

Pubesnes: The soft down on leaves and stems.

Raceme: Unbranched long flower spike on individual stems.

Rhizome: Rootstock; creeping horizontal stem on or below the surface, can have scale or bearing leaves, or aerial shoots towards the tips.

Sepal: A division of the calyx.

Serrate: A sawtooth pattern along the leaf edge.

Spadix: Spike of flowers close around the fleshy axis.

Spathe: Large or pair of bracts enveloping the spadix; also a flower cluster.

Stamen: The male organ, contains the pollen bearing anther and filament.

Stem: Main stalk (or body) of tree, shrub, or plant.

Stigma: The pollen receiving portion of the pistil.

Style: Long narrow portion of the pistil with the stigma at the tip, and ovary below.

Terminal Spike: Borne at the end of a stem.

Trifoliate: Three leaflets per leaf.

Tubers: Underground stem; sometimes covered with modified buds.

Umbel: Flower arrangement originating from the center.

Varigated: Diversity in colour or marks, often in patches or lines.

Notes / Photos / Sketches

Notes / Photos / Sketches

Notes / Photos / Sketches

Notes / Photos / Sketches

Notes / Photos / Sketches

Notes / Photos / Sketches

OFFICIAL WEBSITES FOR THE GEOGRAPHIC AREA COVERED

Anguilla:	*www.anguilla-vacation.com*
Aruba:	*www.aruba.com/home.htm*
Antigua & Barbuda:	*www.antigua-barbuda.org*
Bahamas:	*www.bahamas.com*
Barbados:	*www.barbados.org*
Basseterre includes St Kitts & Nevis:	*www.geographia.com/stkitts-nevis/knpnt02.htm*
Belize:	*www.belize.com*
Bermuda:	*www.bermudatourism.com/docs/index2.html*
Bonaire:	*www.infobonaire.com*
British Virgin Islands & Tortola:	*www.britishvirginislands.com/info.htm*
Costa Rica:	*www.costarica.com*
Cuba:	*www.cuba.com*
Curacao:	*www.geographia.com/curacao*
Dominica:	*www.ndcdominica.dm*
Dominican Republic:	*www.domrep.org*
Florida:	*www.flausa.com*
Georgia:	*www.georgia.org/*
Grand Cayman:	*http://cayman.com.ky/*
Grenada:	*www.geographia.com/grenada*
Guadeloupe:	*www.lonelyplanet.com/destinations/caribbean/guadeloupe*
Guatemala:	*www.guatemala.travel.com*
Haiti:	*www.haiti.org*
Honduras/Roatan:	*www.honduras.com & www.roatanonline.com*
Isla de Cozumel:	*www.islacozumel.com.mx/islacozumel*
Jamaica:	*www.jamaicatravel.com*
Martinique:	*www.touristmartinique.com*
Mexico:	*www.visitmexico.com*
Montserrat:	*www.visitmontserrat.com*
Nicaragua:	*www.nicaragua.com*
Panama:	*www.panamainfo.com*
Puerto Rico:	*http://welcome.topuertorico.org*
Saba:	*www.sabatourism.com*
St. Lucia:	*www.geographia.com/st-lucia*
St. Martin:	*www.geographia.com/st-martin*
St. Vincent:	*www.svgtourism.com*
Trinidad & Tobago:	*www.visittnt.com*
Turks & Caicos:	*www.turksandcaicostourism.com*
US Virgin Islands: St. Croix, St. Thomas, & St. John:	*www.usviguide.com*